SPANISH COLONIAL SILVER

Leona Davis Boylan

Museum of New Mexico Press
In Cooperation With
The International Folk Art Foundation

Photographs in this book by:
Bill Parsons
E. M. Boylan
Robert Dauner

Library of Congress Number 74-82799
ISBN 0-89013-065-5 (hardbound)

ISBN 0-89013-066-3 (softbound)

Published by the Museum of New Mexico Press, Santa Fe, New Mexico.
Printed by Walker Lithocraft, Tucson, Arizona.

TABLE OF CONTENTS

Page

LIST OF FIGURES

INTRODUCTION

The first purpose of this study was to establish the existence of a regional "Northern Provincial"style of Spanish Colonial silver associated with the southwestern part of the United States and to distinguish it stylistically from colonial silver found in other parts of the Spanish New World.

A second purpose was to describe and classify the Spanish Colonial silver in five museum collections in New Mexico: the Sylvanus Griswold Morley Collection, the International Business Machines Collection, the Mrs. Henry Lyman Collection and the Museum of New Mexico Collection—all housed in the latter institution—and the Mary Lester Field Collection in the University Art Museum in Albuquerque.

Interest has been keen and considerable knowledge has been accumulated about colonial silver in New England, but little has been learned about that in the northernmost provinces of New Spain. When one considers the deep and characteristic imprint left by three hundred years of Spanish rule upon vast areas of the United States, especially in New Mexico, it becomes apparent that examination of the little known art of this region can contribute substantially to an understanding of America's artistic heritage. The importance of this kind of study regarding silver work was emphasized when the 1968 Winterthur Conference of the Henry Francis Du Pont Museum chose as its topic, "Spanish, French, and English Traditions in the Colonial Silver of North America."[1]

Since the above mentioned collections had not been examined systematically, it was necessary to begin the present study with firsthand inspection. Each article was photographed along with telescopic details of all hallmarks, monograms, inscription, ranch brands or other identifying characteristics. These were enlarged to approximately twice actual size

1

and mounted with photographs of the piece, or groups of pieces, upon which they were found. Each object was then weighed, measured and described as fully as possible.[2]

Because it is necessary for the reader to be thoroughly acquainted with Spanish Colonial silver as a whole before he can evaluate stylistic distinctions characteristic of the Northern Provincial style, analysis of the New Mexican material—the most important consideration of this study—has been postponed until the last chapter.

In order to facilitate presentation all provincial pieces from rural areas throughout the Spanish Colonial world were brought together to be presented in Chapter VI under the heading, "Provincial Styles." The rest of the material was then divided into three groups according to function: ecclesiastic silver, domestic silver and accessories and gear. These are discussed in Chapters III, IV and V respectively. Thus, earlier chapters provide an analytical basis for isolating a Northern Provincial style within the body of Spanish Colonial provincial silver.

The next step was to identify as many pieces as possible by known hallmarks. Those objects with no identifiable stamps were then subjected to the techniques of stylistic analysis and comparison for the purpose of assigning and dating individual pieces. Where this was not possible, reasonable assumptions were formulated within a framework of historical reference and documentary evidence.

Much identification by hallmarks was made possible by Lawrence Anderson's monumental two volume work *The Art of the Silversmith in Mexico 1519-1936,* in which he published many reproductions of legal marks with the names and dates of Mexican chief assayers and silversmiths who used them throughout the colonial period. In addition to pictures of genuine dies he also provided an invaluable aid for authenticating colonial pieces by reproducing twenty-six stamps which he found being used fraudulently in Mexico City in the 1930s.[3]

Appreciation is acknowledged to the many people who generously helped with the preparation of this study. Interviews with authorities in the fields of Spanish Colonial history and art were most helpful, as were those with individuals whose families still, in many ways, live in the tradition of their forefathers—the Spanish colonizers of New Mexico. Information received from the latter was often anecdotal and could not, therefore, be considered authoritative. Such contacts, however, were an enriching experience which deepened the writer's appreciation both for the works of art and those early New Mexicans who felt it important to bring evidences of their traditional standard of living into an often hostile land.

Special appreciation is extended to the several scholars and museum curators who were helpful with research: to Miss Eleanor Adams, research associate professor of history at the University of New Mexico, for fruitful suggestions and interpretations of old Spanish manuscripts; to Mr. William A. Keleher, noted New Mexican historian and legal adviser to the Field family, for a copy of that part of the Field will which refers to the University of New Mexico collection; to Dr. Ward Alan Minge of Corrales, New Mexico, for permission to include material from his extensive collection of Spanish Colonial documents and art objects; to Lorna Lester Cole and Concha Ortiz y Pino de Kleven for biographical information about Mrs. Field and the Ortiz family; to Dr. Bainbridge Bunting, professor of art at the University of New Mexico, for his constant help and encouragement and to E. Boyd, Curator of Spanish Colonial collections at the Museum of New Mexico, under whose direction the study was made and without whose assistance the task would have been almost impossible.

For the photographs which are so essential to the presentation I am indebted to Mr. Robert Dauner of the University Photographic Service and my own special team of photographers: my son-in-law, Mr. Bill Parsons, and my husband, Mr. E. M. Boylan. Their artistry, skill and patience are greatly appreciated.

FOOTNOTES

[1] *1968 Winterthur Conference Report,* (Winterthur, Delaware: Henry Francis du Pont Museum), 1969.

[2] This material presented in collection catalogues, App. I, pp. 163-179. Weights are not usually included in descriptions of silver plate, but since Spanish Colonial silver is characteristically heavy, they are noted in this study.

[3] All genuine and forged Mexican marks verified by Anderson are reproduced from *The Art of the Silversmith in Mexico 1519–1936,* Vol. I in App. II, pp. 180-196, this study.

CHAPTER I

THE COLLECTIONS

The five collections included in this study contain 329 pieces of silver. In addition, twenty-seven articles in the Fred Harvey Collection (formerly housed in the Alvarado Hotel in Albuquerque) broadened the base to 356 objects available for observation and comparison.[1] Such a concentration of material within a radius of sixty miles provided an invaluable opportunity for a comprehensive study of Spanish Colonial silver in New Mexico.

Quantity, however, was not the only outstanding feature of this material. A breakdown, according to classification and geographic points of origin, revealed an unusually good distribution for comparisons between the various types and styles of silver objects produced in North and South America during the colonial period:

CLASSIFICATIONS
    Ecclesiastic silver 24
    Domestic silver 289
    Accessories and gear...16
POINTS OF ORIGIN
    Peru 9
    Chile 1
    Mexico...187
    (includes two early 20th century reproductions)
    Ecuador..1
    Bolivia...14
    Colombia 8

Forty-four articles from the above distribution are so strikingly different from those known to have been manufactured in cosmopolitan centers that it seems they originated in rural areas and can be classified as provincial. Of this group, twenty-three are from the northern provinces of colonial Mexico which are now part of the United States. The other twenty-one were made in present-day Mexico, Bolivia, Colombia, Argentina and the San Blas Islands off the north coast of Panama. Thus we have a representative group of provincial objects (discussed in Chapter VI) for comparison with each other and with nonprovincial pieces of the same type in order to identify a hitherto unrecognized Northern Provincial style of Spanish Colonial silver. This kind of classification was deemed desirable in regard to the provincial style of northwest Argentina, which developed under many of the same conditions that prevailed in Colonial New Mexico. It is called *Norteño* (northern style) or *Norteña* (northern silver) by A. Taullard and other authorities to distinguish it from the style of Buenos Aires and its environs.[2]

Future investigation of Spanish Colonial silver in the United States may disprove conclusions reached from the study of so small a group as the present one. It seems likely, however, that these forty-four objects, because of their variety and distribution, constitute a good representative sample which can be studied with results that would not be significantly different if many more pieces were available for examination.

Distribution within the combined collections, of course, represents the tastes and circumstances of the various collectors. But it also reflects important differences between the northern frontier provinces of colonial Mexico and other parts of the Spanish New World. One would expect New Mexican collections to have fewer pieces of ecclesiastic silver than those from regions with many richly appointed churches. Also, a comparable group of objects assembled in populous areas more affluent than New Mexico would undoubtedly include more personal accessories, especially jewelry and decorations for bridles, saddles and harness.

Regional differences do not account entirely for the high percentage of domestic silver in the collections. It results, in part, because three collectors, Dr. Sylvanus Griswold Morley, Mrs. Henry Lyman and Mrs. Mary Lester Field, were primarily interested in assembling table services for their own homes. For example, of the ninety-four pieces in the Field Collection eighty-nine are for domestic use with only three for the church and two for personal wear. This collection is particularly important historically because it is the only one of the five which was assembled entirely in New Mexico. It therefore contains more objects from this area than the other four. Fifteen of the twenty-three Northern Provincial articles discussed in Chapter VI were collected by Mrs. Field, who came to New Mexico from Tennessee in 1866 to visit her brother Felix Hill Lester, a young lawyer who had established a practice in Albuquerque. She stayed to become the wife of a fellow attorney, Neill Brooks Field, who was to become mayor of the growing frontier city in 1893–94. Collecting regional art objects soon became one of the abiding interests of her life, especially pieces of massive table silver like those from which she was served by Spanish-speaking friends. She also collected *santos* (holy images) and other Spanish Colonial and Indian objects, many of which were given to the University of New Mexico by the trustees of her estate after her death on February 16, 1933.[3]

Mrs. Field wrote notes on the backs of photographs of pieces in her collection which indicate the eagerness with which she searched out-of-the-way places for her treasures. One note describes how she found a large fluted bowl (Fig. 32-A), made in Mexico at the turn of the nineteenth century by master silversmith Antonio Caamaño, which was being used as a watering dish for chickens in Peña Blanca, a little town north of Albuquerque. Unfortunately, she neither signed nor dated her notes; thus, although they provided some fruitful leads for investigation, they cannot be accepted as impeccable historical data. According to Willima A. Keleher, noted Albuquerque historian and legal adviser to Mrs. Field, she spent over forty years, probably between the 1890s and the 1930s, assembling her silver collection.[4]

The Sylvanus Griswold Morley Collection in the Museum of New Mexico in Santa Fe was the largest of the five. It consisted of 133 pieces of domestic silver. Dr. Morley, for many years dean of Maya scholars in the United States, and his wife assembled most of the silver service in Guatemala while he conducted archeological studies for the Carnegie Institution of Washington. He gave the collection to the Museum of New Mexico while serving as director until his death in 1948. The collection was intact when this study was made. In 1970 part of this was returned to Morley heirs. All pieces no longer in the MNM collection are marked with an asterisk where they are mentioned in the text.

The Museum of New Mexico Collection contains seventy pieces from ten countries. Forty-one items were made for domestic use, fifteen for the church, seven for trappings or gear and seven for personal use. Such diversity results, in part, from the generosity of individuals who have contributed to the collection throughout the years since the museum's founding in 1909. Two especially, Miss Mary Cabot Wheelwright and Miss M. V. Conkey, merit special appreciation for the number and quality of their gifts.[5]

Miss Wheelwright, a Bostonian, proved her concern for the preservation of the artistic heritage of New Mexico by founding the Museum of Navaho Ceremonial Art in Santa Fe in 1937. She also served the Museum of New Mexico well when she persuaded her cousin, Mrs. Henry Lyman, to donate fifteen pieces of domestic silver to the department of Spanish Colonial Art. Mrs. Lyman's collection was assembled in Mexico and South America, mostly in Colombia, where she lived while her husband worked as an engineer on the Panama Canal between 1903 and 1914. Fortunately for the purposes of this study, the Lyman Collection includes four objects from rural Colombia which were exceedingly valuable for comparison with provincial pieces from other parts of the Spanish Colonial Empire.

Miss Conkey came to Santa Fe in the 1920s as a patient in the world-famous Sunmount Sanitarium then situated a short distance from the city in the foothills of the Sangre de Cristo Mountains on the Old Pecos Road. She bought objects of artistic and historic interest from local residents who brought them to the sanitarium to sell to the patients and staff and she continued to collect, especially during the Depression years of the 1930s, when many families were willing to sell. Her gifts are particularly valuable to this study because so many were obtained locally.

The fifth collection was given to the Museum of New Mexico by the International Business Machines Corporation in 1961. It consists of seventeen choice articles collected about thirty years ago by agents of the company in Paraguay, Bolivia, Peru, Chile and Argentina. Five of the six pieces of ecclesiastic silver are of the rare, ornate Jesuit Mission style of Paraguay and four articles for domestic use are *Norteño*. Without the latter, that part of the study dependent upon comparing provincial styles would have been impossible.

Only 187 articles in the combined collections originated in Mexico or New Mexico and so are directly related to the historic past of the state. The rest, from all parts of the Spanish Colonial world, represent national and regional styles which differed then as they do today. The good fortune of being able to compare so many styles, from so many different places, cannot be overemphasized. It is precisely because of the variety in these five collections that a meaningful study of Spanish Colonial silver in New Mexico was possible.

FOOTNOTES

[1] At the time of writing, the Alvarado Hotel was being demolished. The Fred Harvey Collection of Spanish Colonial and Indian art objects was divided and sent (on long term loan) to the Heard Museum in Phoenix and The Museum of Northern Arizona, in Flagstaff and the Museums of New Mexico and Navaho Ceremonial Art, both in Santa Fe.

[2] The word *Norteño* is used in this study to designate this particular style.

[3] A complete list of items left to the university as set forth in the text of the receipt and agreement signed by the trustees of the Mary Lester Field estate and the Board of Regents of the University of New Mexico on May 6, 1939, included in App. III, p. 197 this study.

[4] William A. Keleher, *Turmoil in New Mexico, 1846–1868,* (Santa Fe, New Mexico: Rydal Press, 1952), p. 128.

[5] All donors and those who have pieces on loan to the Museum of New Mexico are credited in catalogue descriptions, App. I, pp. 163-179 this study.

CHAPTER II

HISTORICAL BACKGROUND IN NEW MEXICO

Silver for use in homes and churches was intimately related to colonial life in New Mexico. In fact, because some of the first settlers brought articles with them, the history of Spanish Colonial silver dates from the beginnings of European colonization in the United States.

On May 4, 1598, Don Juan de Oñate crossed the Rio Grande at *El Paso del Norte,* a ford at the present site of Juarez, Mexico, and El Paso, Texas. With him were the first colonists authorized by the Spanish crown to enter what is now the United States for the purpose of establishing homes and transplanting the social, civil and religious forms of the Old World to that part of the New.[1]

Over two hundred colonists, many with their families (including, in some cases, grandchildren and in-laws), were in the group which left the province of Santa Bárbara on the southern border of the modern state of Chihuahua for New Mexico, some eight hundred miles to the north. They were accompanied by eight Franciscan friars and two lay brothers whose mission it was to establish churches and convert the aborigines of the new land. They traveled with about eighty *carretas* (two-wheeled ox-carts), herded some seven thousand head of cattle and drove a train of pack mules loaded with household goods, farm implements, tools, clothing and other supplies.[2]

Before leaving Mexico they were subjected to a series of inspections which, typical of the policy of Spain and its colonial bureaucracy, listed everything each was taking to the new land. The final inventory (the Salazar inspection) began on December 22, 1597, near the San Gerónimo river a few miles from Santa Bárbara. In it, Don Juan and three others declared silver articles of various types.[3] Captain Francisco de Sosa Peñalosa, Alférez Real (Royal Ensign) of the army, said that he was taking "seven hundred pesos [about fifty-six dollars on today's exchange but representing a much greater purchasing value then] worth of silver articles for my personal use." Captain Juan Gutiérrez Bocanegra, commander of the fortress to be built in New Mexico, claimed "one salt shaker [probably a small salt dish] and a small silver pitcher." Don Alonso de Sosa Alvarez Albornoz stated, "this declaration does not include my silks, clothes, silver, or jewels or those of the Doña Beatriz Navarro, my wife . . . ."[4]

Oñate mentions articles of gear which had been described in an earlier inventory of his goods (Ulloa inspection) on January 28, 1597: ". . . six saddles, one with embroidered blue velvet trappings, with spurs and poitrels [armor used to protect a war horse] of silver. . . ."[5] Historian Cleve Hallenbeck, after listing scores of articles Don Juan was required by contract to supply for personal use, stated, "Nothing was said of a silver dining service, which probably was taken for granted; at any rate other traveling officials had it."[6]

Although specific references to silver were not set forth in the inventories of other traveling officials, it is probable that a number of those who stated that their declarations did not include clothing, silks, linens and other items for personal use sometimes referred to silver table services, for these were important status symbols in Spanish Colonial society.

These colonists were different from many American pioneers who were to settle the western frontiers some three hundred years later. Oñate's company included several men of wealth and position with their families and servants, adventurous young *caballeros* intent on advancing themselves financially and socially, officers, soldiers, artisans and, of course, a number of people with nothing but a desire to make a new start in a new land.

Some items listed in the inventories seem frivolous when considered with the knowledge of hindsight about actual conditions under which the colony was to struggle. However, when one remembers the riches which had almost immediately rewarded *conquistadores* in Mexico and Peru, it is easy to understand why some colonists felt it important to bring status symbols of wealth and class to New Mexico, where they hoped to find the same kind of rewards. That silver services were high on the list of such symbols is obvious when one compares the value of Don Francisco de Sosa Peñalosa's "seven hundred pesos worth" of silver with other items in the inspection lists: six pairs of cordovan shoes, valued at nine pesos, and three pairs of bridles and spurs of good quality, at six pesos.[7]

The colony moved north from El Paso, following the Rio Grande except for a dreaded ninety mile strip of desert later called "*Jornada del Muerte*" (Journey of Death), which had to be crossed because rough terrain made a river route impossible. On July 11, 1598, the leading contingent arrived at the first permanent homesite, the Indian Pueblo of Ohke on the east bank of the Rio Grande about twenty-five miles north of Santa Fe. This settlement, which they called San Juan de los Caballeros, was abandoned for San Gabriel del Yunque, a pueblo on the west bank of the Rio Grande, sometime between the spring of 1599 and July, 1600. Here, at San Gabriel, they lived until the capital was moved to Santa Fe in 1610 by Pedro de Peralta, Oñate's successor as governor of the province of New Mexico.

On Christmas Eve of the year 1600, seventy-three new recruits arrived from Mexico City to reinforce the garrison of San Gabriel. With them was one Captain Antonio Conde de Herrera with his wife, children, brothers and sisters-in-law. Among the effects of his wife, Doña Francisca Galindo, were "two pitchers; a small pot and a saltcellar of silver, with six small and one large spoons." The new arrivals also brought "one sword and one dagger, silver plated, with belts and straps trimmed with gold and green and red" for Governor Oñate.[8]

It is impossible to know what happened to the sixteenth century silver owned by these first New Mexicans. Some may still belong to their descendents, many of whom still live in the state, but most of it probably has been lost, sold or destroyed.[9] According to E. Boyd, curator of Spanish Colonial collections for the Museum of New Mexico, many families sold their silver at pound value during the early Territorial period (1846–1862) when, because of unfamiliarity with American business practices, formerly well-to-do New Mexicans lost their lands and possessions to the newcomers.

Some articles were undoubtedly sold to people who took them out of the state. We can be sure that Miss Conkey was not the only person who bought from families who needed to raise cash during the Depression years of the early twentieth century, or that others had not done so in times past. We have the record of one such incident when Governor Manuel Armijo collected his wealth and fled before the United States Army as it entered Santa Fe on August 18, 1846. By 1850 he was living on one of his properties at Lemitar, where he was so short of cash that he was "forced to offer his silver table service to an American lieutenant for three hundred dollars."[10]

11

A few of the objects examined in this study might be sixteenth century but, since none is stamped with marks used in Mexico at that time, this cannot be proved.[11] However, Edward Wenham, foremost authority on old silver, believes that several of the mugs in the Field Collection are actually very old beakers to which handles were added at a later date.[12]

As one reads chronicles of the Spanish conquest in America he becomes increasingly convinced that missionary zeal was one of its most powerful motivating forces—as strong to some as the desire for wealth and power. Most of the conquerors and colonizers believed absolutely that Spain was the divinely appointed instrument of God's will for the propagation of the Roman Catholic faith. To them, the New World was one vast missionary field, to be conquered and pacified under the banner of *Los Dos Reyes* (The Two Kings)—God and King. With each group entering new territory throughout Spanish America went members of one of the teaching and preaching monastic orders who time and again risked their lives and endured almost inconceivable hardships, particularly during the early years, in pursuit of their mission. Where Spain went, churches were built. The history of Spanish Colonial art would be impoverished indeed if this were not true.

Though the missions of New Mexico never approached the splendor of churches in many parts of Mexico and South America, they were then, as they are now, the pride of the pueblos and Spanish towns. Most decorations and furnishings were made locally of materials less precious than silver, but a few articles, especially those used in Holy Communion, were brought from Mexico. Eleven silver chalices and patens were inventoried among the supplies brought to Santa Fe in 1626 by Fray Alonso Benavides, custodian and commissary of the Holy Inquisition, who came with twelve Franciscan friars to join the fourteen already there. An entry in the record of his inspection reads:

> Thirty-eight marks and four ounces of silver, which was the weight of 11 chalices, with gold-plated patens, and the chalices plated likewise inside, with engraved base, at 3 marks and 4 ounces each, at 65 reales the mark . . . 312 pesos, 6 ts., 6 gr.
>
> For the gold and the making of the above 11 chalices, at 24 pesos each . . . 264 pesos
>
> Eleven missals, recently revised, bound, at 15 pesos each . . . 165 pesos
>
> Eleven pairs of brass candleholders, at 3 pesos per pair . . . 33 pesos
>
> Eleven pairs of snuffing scissors, at 3 tomines per pair . . . 4 pesos, 1 tn.[13]

Obviously, Benavides was supplying eleven missions with chalices and patens for the bread and wine of the Eucharist. By church law these articles were required to be made of precious metal with the insides—that part which comes in contact with the Elements—covered with gold. Engravings mentioned were probably identification inscriptions. Since they were destined for use in frontier mission churches they were no doubt simple in design, somewhat like a provincial chalice in the Museum of New Mexico collection (Fig. 58), which is gold-washed rather than gold plated on the inside. The last item listed above is interesting because it proves that candle snuffers were made in the form of scissors, like one in the Morley Collection* (Fig. 53-B), as early as the beginning of the seventeenth century. Their price, eleven pairs for a fraction more than four pesos, indicates that they were made of brass to match the candle-holders.

Evidently the realities of frontier life were still not comprehended by officials in Mexico by the middle of the seventeenth century for, according to Manuel T. Espinosa, "Some of the governors tried to bring with them the trappings of wealth and position. Governor Mendizábal [Bernardo Lopez de, 1659–1661] and his wife brought a carriage, a fine bed and hangings, gilded writing desks, silver plate, expensive clothes. . . ."[14] It is doubtful that any of their silver remained in New Mexico because all of the governor's personal property was shipped to Parral in the present state of Chihuahua when he and his wife were recalled to Mexico City for trial before the Holy Inquisition in 1663.[15] Some may have been sold in the *tienda* (store) which he, one of the greediest and most enterprising of New Mexican colonial governors, had established in Santa Fe.

In August of 1680 northern New Mexico was ravaged by a revolt of the Pueblo Indians under the leadership of a Shaman from San Juan named Po-Pé. It was a well organized attack which took the colonists by surprise, particularly in outlying areas where isolated settlers were slaughtered before they could reach the protection of the towns. It seems little short of a miracle that any were able to escape to the south, leaving the northern settlements in a condition graphically described by C. W. Hackett in *Historical Documents Relating to New Mexico Nueva Vizcaya and Approaches Thereto* which was published by the Carnegie Institution of Washington in 1923–27:

> The condition of New Mexico now beggared description. From Taos to Isleta, a distance of fifty leagues [about 130 miles] the whole country was devastated and depopulated. The *estancias* and *haciendas* of the Spanish settlers had been robbed of both household goods and of the

horses and cattle of the fields, while many of the houses had been burned. The churches, where not burned, had been stripped of their sacred vessels, robbed of their ornament, and in every way as completely and foully desecrated as Indian sacrilege and indecency could suggest, while the sacred vestments had been made use of by the Indians as trophies in the dances and festivities celebrating their success. But sadder and more serious than this was the number that had been killed. Throughout the entire province it had been the aim of the Indians to totally exterminate the Spaniards, and consequently no mercy was shown . . . not even to the child at the breast nor to the zealous *Padre* who administered the Holy Faith.[16]

Statistics of the revolt reveal that the colony's population had multiplied many times since the first settlement. Records show that over twenty-five hundred refugees escaped from Santa Fe and Isleta Pueblo (the only one which did not join the massacre) and about two thousand arrived at San Lorenzo, a few miles north of El Paso, after burying hundreds of their dead in the *Jornada del Muerte*.[17] These figures indicate that something like three thousand colonists had entered the province since 1600. There can be little doubt that the more well-to-do brought silver dinner services and household articles with them. The only reason to suppose that any pieces were saved during the revolt would be to assume that the Indians kept them. Though unlikely, this is possible, because, although they had not yet learned the art of silversmithing, there is ample evidence later of their love and respect for the white metal.

A little over twelve years later seven hundred colonists returned to northern New Mexico under the leadership of Governor General Don Diego de Vargas Ponce de León Zapata y Luján, reconqueror of New Mexico. De Vargas served as governor of the province until his death on April 8, 1704. We know that he, and probably others, brought in silver plate because he described seventy-five individual items in the will he signed in Bernalillo, where he died after becoming ill while fighting Apaches in the nearby Sandia Mountains.

Descriptions in the de Vargas will are fuller than in most early documents, but even so, they must be discounted to some extent. For example, it states that a large *fuente* (tray) weighed twenty-three Spanish marks.[18] This means, figured by Anderson's table of equivalents, that it weighed well over twelve pounds![19] When one considers that the largest tray in the present collections (Fig. 61-B), which is 62 cm. (2 feet 4 inches) long and 46 cm. (a foot and a half) wide, weighs only 2.35 kg. (5 pounds 3 ounces), the above figure must be suspect. It is possible, since the

14

governor was away from home when he died, that he depended on an understandably unreliable memory in describing his silverware.

He identified forty-three articles as "sealed with my coat-of-arms" and fifty-nine with "the fifth taken." Presumably the former referred to a small die of his family crest (Fig. 1-A). The latter (a tax mark) would have been like one of those which, according to Anderson, were most likely to have been used in Mexico during the sixteenth and seventeenth centuries (Fig. 1-B). The one used before 1578 was probably the first one on the left in the illustration, a crude "M" with a small "o" connecting the diagonals. The other two are Columns of Hercules crowned, an adaptation of the Spanish Arms, with an "M" between which stood for Mexico. Any of these signified that the *quinto real* (royal fifth), a twenty per cent tax imposed on all silver objects made in the colonies, had been paid.[20] Don Diego instructed his attorney and executor, Don Juan Paez Hurtado, to "remit or to sell [his silver] at the best obtainable prices."[21]

It is entirely possible that people living in New Mexico at the time of de Vargas' death bought some of his silver. No pieces examined in this study are stamped with either his coat-of-arms or one of the early Mexican tax marks, but the description of a "large plain tankard, weighing two marks and six ounces" (a little over one and a half pounds), fits that of the largest mug in the Field Collection (Fig. 43). It weighs 765.45 gr. (1 pound 11 ounces), is perfectly plain, is large enough to be called a "tankard" and has a typical seventeenth century form.[22]

Additional supportive evidence that it may indeed be the de Vargas mug was provided by the note Mrs. Field wrote on the back of a photograph of her piece. It says that she got it from Don Salomón Luna of Los Lunas, New Mexico, whose ancestors were among the refugees of 1680 who returned to northern New Mexico with de Vargas in 1693.[23] Obviously, one of them could have bought Don Diego's tankard from his executor in 1704 and the Luna family could have kept it until Mrs. Field acquired it for her collection some two hundred years later.

Two wills executed in Santa Fe early in the nineteenth century testify to the continued popularity of silver dinner services during the eighteenth century. They are those of Captain Don Antonio José Ortiz, signed on August 12, 1806, and his widow, Doña Rosa Bustamante, who died in 1814. Don Antonio listed 132 pieces of tableware, eighty-four of which he specified as *"con quintos"* (with tax stamps). Included was practically everything needed to serve thirty people. In his wife's will the total number was increased to 144 items and the distribution differed slightly. She identified 123 articles as having tax stamps and nineteen as "ordinary," or without tax marks. Two tantaluses, probably only decorated with silver, were not described either way.[24]

A. DE VARGAS COAT-OF-ARMS

B. SIXTEENTH CENTURY MEXICAN MARKS

Figure 1

BAR OF BULLION

Figure 2

16

The Ortíz family was one of the wealthiest in colonial New Mexico, with holdings in Santa Fe and scattered throughout the province as far south as El Paso. Don Antonio, who served as *alcalde* and *Alfériz Real* of the *Villa* of Santa Fe, acted for the crown in the tradition of his forefathers, the first of whom was cited for military valor in 1697 by Governor de Vargas.[25] Some of the Ortíz silver may have been seventeenth century or earlier, but most was probably made in the eighteenth century. Members of the family had ample opportunity to buy while traveling in the interests of their business, or to import articles on the supply trains which arrived every three years over the *Camino Real* (Royal Road) from Mexico City.

Mrs. Concha Ortíz y Pino de Kleven, descendent of Don Antonio and Doña Rosa, says that the Ortíz silver has been scattered since these wills were written over a hundred and fifty years ago. Her grandmother, a contemporary of Mary Lester Field, told her that several items in the Field collection were purchased from members of the Ortíz family or others to whom they had been given during the preceding century. She also believes that a few articles in the Museum of New Mexico collection were originally part of the Ortíz family silver.

Trade with French settlements in the Mississippi River country began in 1739 when the Mallet brothers, with six companions, brought a load of goods to Santa Fe. Other French traders, and later the Anglo-Americans, tried to establish trade with New Mexico, especially after the explorations of Zebulon Montgomery Pike in 1805–07. According to Ralph Emerson Twitchell, Pike "gave the people of the United States the first information of a reliable character concerning conditions in Northern Mexico, and his expedition unquestionably was the means of inducing traders to come to New Mexico in quest of profitable returns in business ventures."[26] Because of opposition from the Spanish crown it was not until the 1820s, when independent Mexico was concerned with her own internal problems, that regular trade was established over the Santa Fe Trail to Missouri.

Early American travelers over the trail were impressed by the solid silver table services from which they were served by hospitable New Mexicans. One, a poet-philosopher from New Orleans named Matt Field, wrote of his experiences in a series of articles for the *Times Picayune* in 1841. One vignette, titled "A Mexican Inn," describes a small tavern where he and his party stayed shortly after they left Taos for Santa Fe. It must have been located in the Rio Grande Canyon for he described it as:

> ...situated in a deep and narrow valley, the mountains soaring in the clouds above it on every side. It stood upon the banks of the Rio

Grande, so near the mountain source of that noble river, that we could find no greater depth of water than four inches. . . . The host was a rosy, rotund, hearty old fellow . . . the inn was furnished with, and in all its appointments, displayed more costly elegance and taste, than any other house we entered in this part of Mexico. We were served upon silver plates and dishes, which were laid upon exquisitely wrought Chihuahua blankets, and we sat upon the most luxurious couches. . . .[27]

Another chronicler was with General Stephen Watts Kearney when he annexed New Mexico for the United States in 1846. He was Lieutenant W. H. Emory, who wrote a day-by-day account of the campaign for the government in Washington. When the American Army entered Santa Fe on the eighteenth of August, Kearney and his staff were met by Acting Governor Juan Bautista Vigil and a group of leading citizens, which included young Francisco Perea of Bernalillo, who acted as interpreter for the surrender of the city.

Francisco had learned to speak English while attending a Jesuit college in St. Louis between 1843 and 1845 with his brother Joaquín and several other New Mexican youths. The two brothers, who were among the first to receive their educations in the United States instead of Mexico, went east again in the spring of 1847 to enroll in the select Bank Street Academy in New York City where Professor Hincinle Peuhne, formerly a captain in Napoleon's army, was headmaster.[28]

A few weeks after meeting General Kearney in Santa Fe, Don Juan Perea, Francisco's father, entertained the Americans in his home in Bernalillo. Evidently one of the younger Pereas did the same the following day because of this occasion Emory wrote:

We passed on to the house of our host's wealthy son, where we were invited to dine. Here we found another refreshment table; and after waiting some hours, dinner was announced. It was a queer jumble of refinement and barbarism; the first predominating in everything, except the mode of serving, which was chiefly performed by the master, his Mexican guests, and a few female serfs. The plates, forks, and spoons were of solid New Mexican silver, clumsily worked in the country.[29]

Emory's assumption that the silver was made in the country indicates that at least part of it was provincial in style. According to Keleher, this table service was divided among many descendents of the family and "Mary Lester Field, of Albuquerque, devoted more than forty years to locating and acquiring the scattered Perea silver-ware."[30] There is no documentary proof that any of Mrs. Field's pieces were actually those that Emory saw, but his description, "clumsily worked in the country" suggests that some of her provincial objects may have belonged to the Pereas.

Another American officer, Lieutenant J. W. Abert, was struck by the incongruity of expensive furnishings in what were, to him, the uncomfortable adobe houses which he described in his *Examinations of New Mexico in the Years 1846–47:*

> The houses throughout the country are furnished with mattresses, doubled up and arranged close to the walls, so as to answer for seats; these are covered with beautiful Navajoe blankets, worth from 50 to 100 dollars . . . the whole interior of the houses of the wealthy is covered with mirrors. All the hildagos [sic] pride themselves on allowing nothing but silver to approach their tables; even the plates are of silver. But, with all this air of wealth, true comfort is wanting; and very few of our blessed land would consent to live like the wealthiest Rico in New Mexico.[31]

There is no mention of professional *plateros* (silversmiths) in New Mexico prior to the nineteenth century. This does not mean, however, that silver was not worked in the province before that time. Even if there were no professional smiths there is a good probability that silver articles were made on the *haciendas* (ranches) by the blacksmiths who were a necessary part of the work force. This happened on the great ranches of northwestern Argentina and the same conditions which induced home manufacturing there, vast distances and limited communication with metropolitan centers, prevailed in New Mexico.[32] A blacksmith, familiar with the problems of hammering and shaping metal, could make perfectly usable silver plates, bowls and cups, especially if he were given objects to copy. This could account for some of the crudities and naive stylistic expressions which delight us in silver collected in New Mexico.

The manufacture of silver wares in New Mexico would have been limited by the fact that there were no mines within the present boundaries of the state until 1867, when one was discovered near Socorro. Bars of bullion, however, bearing the royal insignia of Spain, "R HS ET ID" (*Rex Hispania* of the Indies), with a crude shield and quarterings in the middle, have been found in the state. The one photographed (Fig. 2) is from the collection of Dr. and Mrs. Ward Alan Minges of Corrales. Incidentally, according to E. Boyd, these ingots are being copied now by enterprising curio dealers in New Mexico and Arizona. However, during colonial times silver for fabrication was available in El Paso, then almost in the center of the territory under the jurisdiction of the governor of New Mexico. Hallenbeck, in his description of Indian disturbances in the 1680s says, "The three years of Indian warfare . . . accentuated by a severe drought in 1684, had left the people of the El Paso district impoverished. The Indians had destroyed much property including three silver smelters. . . ."[33]

Good evidence that at least one silversmith was working in Santa Fe early in the nineteenth century was found recently in southern Nebraska. It is an Indian peace medal (Fig. 3) inset with a Spanish coin dated 1791 which, according to Zebulon Pike, was part of the equipment of a military expedition outfitted in Santa Fe in 1806. When the Spanish government learned of Pike's explorations it grew fearful of its enterprising neighbor and sent a military expedition with orders to prevent the Americans from entering New Mexico. According to Pike's own account:

> Lieutenant Don Facundo Malgares [Melgares], the officer selected from the five internal provinces to command this expedition . . . had distinguished himself in several long expeditions against the Apaches and other Indian nations with whom the Spaniards were at war. . . . This officer marched from the province of Biscay with 100 dragoons of the regular service, and at Santa Fe, the place where the expedition was fitted out, he was joined by 500 of the mounted militia of that province, armed after the manner described by my notes on that subject, and completely equipped with ammunition, etc., for six months: each man leading with them (by orders) two horses and one mule, the whole number of their beasts was 2,075. They descended the Red river 233 leagues; met the grand bands of the Tetaus [Comanches] . . . then struck off N.E., and crossed the country . . . to the Pawnee republic. Here he was met by the chiefs and warriors of the Grand Pawnees; held councils with the two nations and presented them the flags, medals, etc., which were destined for them.[34]

According to Elliot Coues' annotation of Pike's account, the site of Melgares' council with the chiefs of the Grand Pawnees was probably that marked on Gregg's map of 1844 as "Old Pawnee Village," across the Republican River from the present town of Red Cloud, Webster County, Nebraska.[35] It is therefore reasonable to assume that this medal, which was found in this area, was presented to a Pawnee chief by Melgares about a month before Pike's arrival in September, 1806.

INDIAN PEACE MEDAL (two views)
Property of the Nebraska Historical Society, Lincoln, Nebraska

Figure 3

One of the purposes of the Melgares expedition was to strengthen Spanish relations with Indian tribes on the periphery of New Mexico. Among the supplies he took from Santa Fe were flags and medals for chiefs of the tribes. These medals were highly prized by the Indians, especially those presented by the Spanish or the English, which seem to have been not only much larger (most of the Spanish ones were four or five inches in diameter), but also to have been distributed with greater discrimination than those of the Americans.[36] A description of a ceremony in New Orleans in 1769 illustrates the importance attached to the presentation of such medals:

> He assured the Indians of the punctuality of the annual presents, and that the King did not wish to demand . . . any other gratitude than . . . constant fidelity. In the afternoon he would parade all the troops of the garrison. At the end of the speech, His Excellency arose from his chair to place about the neck of each . . . of the chiefs the medal which hung from a silk ribbon of deep scarlet color. He first had them kiss the royal effigy, and then with his bare sword he touched them on both shoulders and chest, and made over their heads the sign of the Cross, and finally gave each an embrace, whereupon they again showed . . . that it was evident how pleasing to them was the ceremony. . . .[37]

The royal effigy mentioned was probably on a coin like that of Charles IV on the medal found in Nebraska. It is possible that Melgares brought it from Mexico, but it seems likely, considering its style of decoration and the quality of workmanship (note the suspension ring), that it was made in Santa Fe.

The Ortíz will of 1814 contains contributing evidence of a New Mexican *platero* in Santa Fe at this time. In it Doña Rosa stated, "I declare that I have paid the silversmith for making a reliquary and two silver crowns [probably for statues of the Virgin]."[38] Since she did not name the *platero*, or tell where the crowns and reliquary were made, this evidence is not conclusive. Considered, however, in conjunction with the peace medal, it certainly suggests that the *señora* employed a local silversmith.

Three recruits are described as *plateros* in the army enlistment personnel files in the New Mexico Records and Archives for the first half of the nineteenth century. They were: Francisco de la Peña, Santa Fe, 1828; Tomas S. Sandoval, Santa Fe, 1833 and José Francisco Lópes, Abíquiú, 1842.[39] The second name opens a fascinating area of speculation concerning the identity of our unknown Santa Fe *platero*.

Comparison between the hatched decorations on a pyx (Fig. 60) which was loaned to the Museum of New Mexico by John Sandoval of Santa Fe and those on the peace medal leads to the conjecture that they may have been decorated in the same silver shop. It is hardly possible that they were done by the same hand because workmanship on the medal is far superior to that on the pyx, but the father of the young recruit, Tomas S. Sandoval, might have done the peace medal in 1806 and the younger *platero* the pyx sometime before he was inducted in 1833. The Sandoval family could then have kept it for some 135 years before loaning it to the museum.

The dual role played by a frontier blacksmith is illustrated in a story told to John Adair by a relative of the "Head Chief" who is generally recognized as the first Navajo to learn the art of silversmithing. He was Atsidi Sani (Old Smith), known to New Mexicans as Herrero (iron worker). It tells of how Atsidi Sani went to a blacksmith near Mount Taylor in western New Mexico to learn how to make bridles so he could supply his people, who had been buying from Mexican blacksmiths. The smith, whom the Navajo called Nakai Tsosi (Thin Mexican) "also knew how to work silver." He became Herrero's friend, taught him to make bridles and later, how to fabricate silver.[40] Atsidi Sani also had ample opportunity to watch a silversmith at work in Pass Washington on the Navajo Reservation, where the newly appointed Indian agent, Captain Henry L. Dodge, established a forge in 1853. Another prominent Navajo named Chee Dodge, with whom Herrero lived for many years, said that Herrero had gone to the forge at Pass Washington and "looked on and learned some things."[41]

Captain Dodge stated in a letter written to the editor of the *Santa Fe Weekly Gazette,* dated November 16, 1853, that there were three men working in the forge: an American blacksmith, a Mexican silversmith and an assistant. "I have with me George Carter who is their [the Navjos'] blacksmith, a man of sterling worth and every inch a soldier— a Mexican silversmith, an assistant, Juan Anea, my interpreter, and two Mexican servants."[42] Whether Juan Anea was the name of the assistant smith or Captain Dodge's interpreter is a little hard to determine.

Coins were used for the manufacture of silver articles by both Mexican and Indian *plateros* in the late nineteenth century. One instance is documented in the reminiscences of Mrs. Henrika Busch Huning, a pioneer whose daughter, Mrs. F. C. W. Pooler, preserved her memoirs in a series of notes on frontier life. These were organized by Miss Laurel E. Drew in a paper written for the University of New Mexico in 1963. One anecdote reads:

Principal families in the Los Lunas area were the Lunas, Jaramillo, and Romero. . . . The oldest silverware consisted of silver plates, water pitchers, mugs, trays, hammered from silver dollars by a silversmith in Pajarito. (Anastasio Burgos was the silversmith in Pajarito).[43]

The above documentary evidence proves that there is a provenance of Spanish Colonial silver in New Mexico. The problem, then, is to prove that silver objects fabricated in this northern part of colonial New Spain are stylistically distinctive enough and consistent enough to justify classification. This is the problem to be considered in Chapter VI of this study.

FOOTNOTES

[1]St. Augustine, Florida, predates the New Mexico colony by 33 years, but it was a military garrison established to protect Spanish gold ships returning to Spain via Havana, not a colony of settlers.

[2]Complete record of Oñate Expedition, George P. Hammond and Agapito Rey, *Don Juan de Oñate, Colonizer of New Mexico, 1595–1628,* 2 vols. (Albuquerque: University of New Mexico Press, 1953.)

[3]Ibid., Vol. I, op. cit., pp. 197-308.

[4]Ibid., pp. 239, 241 & 247.

[5]Ibid., p. 136.

[6]Cleve Hallenbeck, *Land of the Conquistadores* (Caldwell, Idaho: The Caxton Printers, Ltd., 1950), p. 61.

[7]Hammond and Rey, Vol. I, pp. 528-529.

[8]Ibid., pp. 526 & 540.

[9]Consult Fray Angélico Chávez, *Origins of New Mexico Families* (Santa Fe: Historical Society of New Mexico, 1954) and Gilberto Espinosa, "A Guide to New Mexico Genealogical Study" (Special Collections, Zimmerman Library, University of New Mexico, n.d.). (Typescript.)

[10]Paul Horgan, *The Great River,* Vol. II (New York: Rinehart & Co., 1954), p. 788.

[11]See App. II, Fig. 81.

[12]Edward Wenham, "Spanish American Silver in New Mexico," *International Studio,* Vol. 99 (January, 1931), 33.

[13]Frederick Webb Hodge, George P. Hammond and Agapito Rey, *Fray Alonso Benavides Revised Memorial of 1634* (Albuquerque: University of New Mexico Press, 1945), p. 114.

[14]Manuel T. Espinosa, *First Expedition of de Vargas into New Mexico, 1692* (Albuquerque: University of New Mexico Press, 1940), p. 12.

[15]Hallenbeck, p. 131.

[16]Ibid., p. 158.

[17]Ibid., p. 162.

[18]According to Miss Eleanor Adams, paleographer at the University of New Mexico, Twitchell translates *fuente* incorrectly here. It was used to indicate a large tray of the type called a *"charola"* rather than a fountain (its usual meaning).

[19]Table of Equivalents from Lawrence Anderson, *The Art of the Silversmith in Mexico 1519–1936,* Vol. I (New York: Oxford University Press, 1941), p. 120.

[20]Ibid., pp. 288-295.

[21]Complete text of that part of the de Vargas will which refers to silver, App. III, p. 197, this study.

[22]Seymour B. Wyler, *The Book of Old Silver* (New York: Crown Publishers, 1937), pp. 47-48.

[23]Chávez, p. 65.

[24]Complete text of those parts of the Ortíz wills which refer to silver, App. III, p. 198, this study.

[25]Ibid., p. 249.

[26]Ralph Emerson Twitchell, *The Leading Facts of New Mexican History,* Vol. II (Cedar Rapids: The Torch Press, 1911–1917), pp. 92–96.

[27]John E. Sunder (ed.), (collected by Clyde and Mae Porter). *Matt Field on the Santa Fe Trail* (Norman: University of Oklahoma Press, 1960), p. 195.

[28]W. H. H. Allison (Ralph Emerson Twitchell, ed.), "Colonel Francisco Perea," *Old Santa Fe,* I, No. 4 (April, 1914), 212-213.

[29]W. H. Emory, *Lieutenant Emory Reports* (Albuquerque: University of New Mexico Press, 1951), p. 68.

[30]William A. Keleher, *Turmoil in New Mexico, 1846–1866* (Santa Fe: Rydal Press, 1952), p. 128.

[31]J. W. Abert, *Examinations of New Mexico in the Years 1846–47* (House Executive Documents, Thirtieth Congress, First Session, Doc. 41. Washington: Government Printing Office, 1848), p. 452.

[32]E. Boyd, "Colonial Silver from Latin America," *El Palacio,* Vol. 69/2 (1962), 119–123.

[33]Hallenbeck, p. 176.

[34]Elliott Coues (ed. and annot.), *The Expeditions of Zebulon Montgomery Pike,* 3 vols. (New York: Francis P. Harper, 1895), p. 413.

[35]Ibid., p. 410.

[36]Ibid., p. 551.

[37]Richard E. Ahlborn, *Domestic Silver in Colonial Mexico and Comments on Peru*. (1968 Winterthur Conference Report. Winterthur, Delaware: Henry Francis du Pont Museum, 1969), p. 34.

[38]Ortíz *Family Papers,* (Doc. III, Article 43. Santa Fe: State Records and Archives).

[39]Courtesy of Dr. Ward Alan Minges, Corrales, New Mexico.

[40]John Adair, *The Navajo and Pueblo Silversmiths* (Norman: University of Oklahoma Press, 1944), p. 4.

[41]Arthur Woodward, *A Brief History of Navajo Silversmithing* (Flagstaff: Northern Arizona Society of Science and Art, 1946), pp. 15–17.

[42]Ibid.

[43]Laurel E. Drew, ''Henrika (Busch) Huning'' (unpublished paper 29/Y, Albuquerque: University of New Mexico, 1963), p. 2.

CHAPTER III

ECCLESIASTIC SILVER

The selection of silver in these New Mexico collections cannot be considered a typical cross section of Spanish Colonial silver as a whole. One of the chief reasons is the limited number of ecclesiastic pieces compared to domestic. In other areas just as many, if not more, objects were made for use in churches as in homes. This becomes immediately apparent when one notes the preponderance of ecclesiastic silver included in such works as Taullard's *Platería Sudamericana,* or Volume II of Anderson's *Art of the Silversmith in Mexico 1519–1936.*

Although this unusual distribution results in part from preferences of the collectors, it also reflects the relative poverty of New Mexican churches compared to those in Mexico, Central and South America—many of which were decorated and appointed with almost unbelievable splendor. As mentioned earlier, the church required that certain sacramental vessels be made of precious metals, and preferred the same for many other objects. These were favored gift items from wealthy parishioners to churches throughout Spanish America. Thousands upon thousands of exquisitely wrought gold and silver objects, ranging in importance from ornate tabernacles and altar fronts to tiny ornaments for holy images, are preserved in Spanish American colonial churches.

Expensive appointments, however, would have ill fitted the nature and function of New Mexico's mission churches. These were simple adobe buildings consisting of a long narrow nave, usually with a *coro* (choir balcony) over the main entrance, and a hexagonal apse at the opposite end. They were often decorated with painted *retablos* (flat wall decorations) behind the altars, carved figures of the saints called *bultos* and, in some instances, colorful dados and ceiling designs. The missions were founded by the Franciscans who, like their founder, St. Francis of Assisi, held vows of poverty and worked among the lowly of the earth. Except for a few in Spanish towns along the river, most of their thirty-seven churches were located in Indian pueblos where some friars continued to serve until 1820, even though they had been gradually withdrawn and replaced by the secular clergy after 1798.

The church was the center of a mission complex which included a *convento* (convent) with quarters, shops, storerooms, and corrals arranged around an open court where much mission activity took place. Outside were kitchen gardens, fields for crops and pastures for livestock. Each mission was a school where blacksmithing, carpentry, leather working, the household arts and agriculture were taught in addition to the precepts of the Holy Faith and the Spanish language.[1] It was the working heart of a community, not a symbol of the wealth and power of the church.

As their administration was assumed by seculars, town churches were supplied with somewhat better furnishings. An inventory compiled by Ecclesiastic Visitor Fray Anastasio Dominguez, who toured the Province in 1776, listed many silver articles in the parish church of Santa Fe. His description of the sacristy silver in the Mission Church of St. Thomas in Abiquiú, however, tells a different story, "Chalice with paten and no spoon, but the chalice is in three pieces, and one of them, for it is a loan by the settlers, is used for a little shrine they have. A small ciborium. . . . Pyx for the Viaticum. . . . Cruets and a small bell on their plate. Shell and salt receptacle for baptisms. . . ."[2]

It was not until 1851, when Archbishop Lamy was sent to Santa Fe, that churches in New Mexico began to be appointed with some of the traditional richness of Roman Catholic churches elsewhere. It is understandable, therefore, that most of the ecclesiastic silver in the New Mexico collections originated in distant areas: Mexico, Guatemala, Colombia, Ecuador, Paraguay, Peru, Spain and France.

One of the most impressive examples is a pair of eighteenth century Mexican candlesticks now on a long-term loan to the Museum of New Mexico from the Fred Harvey Collection (Fig. 6). Each is inscribed around its triangular base with the legend *"SON DE LA ARCHCOERA. DADE S. SMO/DE LA YGLESIA DE ESTA NUEBA BERA CRUZ/ ANO DE 1729."* E. Boyd translates this archaic Spanish as, "These are of the choirmaster, given by His Holiness *(Su Santisimo)*/ of the church of this New Vera Cruz/year of 1729."

In 1599 the city of Vera Cruz, Mexico, was moved from the swampy area where it had been established by Cortés in 1519. The term "New Vera Cruz" was then used for some two centuries to distinguish the new site from the old. It is impossible to know the particular church in the new city to which the inscriptions refer, but the elegance of these candlesticks indicates that they were probably part of the furnishings of an important church, possibly the cathedral. In 1729 the appelation "His Holiness" was not reserved in Mexico exclusively for the Pope, as it is today, but was often used simply for priests. The choirmaster himself would have been a priest in charge of choir furnishings, so the legend could refer to him without necessarily indicating that the objects were his personal property.

Each candlestick consists of six separate parts on a steel center rod: a triangular base with acanthus leaf corners, a flat lid which fits over the base, a turned stem, the flared lower section of the candle-base, the upper half of the candle-base and a candleholder (bobêche). All parts are held together by a silver wing-nut tightened under the base.

Three Mexican marks, "LIN" over "CR," a Mundos y Mares and an eagle, are stamped on each of the twelve separate parts. According to Anderson the initials "LIN" over "CR" are forgeries of those of Chief Assayer José Antonio Lince González, who served between 1779 and 1788 (App. II, Fig. 87, No. 8-E). It would seem, however, that he must be wrong on this point for there is absolutely no doubt that these candlesticks, dated fifty years before Lince González held office, are genuine.

Although some of the marks are worn from time and use, all are perfectly legible. Furthermore, both pieces have all the characteristics of fine old silver: extraordinary weight, a soft blue-white patina, evidence of wear and the excellent design and craftsmanship typical of eighteenth century work. They are stamped with the two marks required by law between 1638 and 1732: a tax stamp (eagle) and an artisan's mark. The third mark, a Mundos y Mares, is a rare stamp which Anderson also declared a forgery:

This forgery merits special mention. Almost from the beginning of the Conquest the arms of Spain were stamped on precious metals and a shield bearing the same arms appeared on money coined in Mexico called macuquina (applied to coins with the milled edges cut away), until the year 1732. From that date to 1771 money was coined called Columnaria ó de Mundos y Mares (Columnar or of Land and Seas), the reverse side of which was not changed during this period.

29

Probably through ignorance false marks were made bearing the shield of *Mundos y Mares*. There were no genuine marks bearing this device.[3]

Again it appears that Anderson was mistaken. A *Mundos y Mares* was stamped here, probably as a hallmark of quality, on genuine old silver dated in 1729, three years before the date he gives for the beginning of its use on coins.

It is easy to understand how such mistakes were made. The number of marks alone would indicate a date between 1733 and 1782. In 1732 laws controlling the stamping of silver were changed to include the mark of the chief assayer in order to signify that the metal was of the required standard (hallmark of quality). Between 1638 and 1732 a single stamp, besides the silversmith's mark, had stood for both the tax and the standard of metal. In 1782 the law was changed again. Between 1782 and 1820 four marks were required—those of the previous period plus a place mark for Mexico ("M" surmounted by a crown).[4] After Mexico became independent in 1821 the marks remained the same except that the crown over the "M" was replaced by a small "o." We can only speculate as to why three marks were stamped on these candlesticks in 1729, three years before that number was required by law.

The initials "LIN" over "CR" would have been as confusing as the number of marks because of their similarity to those of Chief Assayer Lince González, "LIN" over "CE" (App. II, Fig. 85, Nos. 7 & 8). This was especially true since there is no record of another early eighteenth century assayer or silversmith whose name could have been contracted in this manner. It was reasonable, therefore, to assume that they were forgeries of the Lince González mark—an assumption which would then have seemed a certainty when Anderson found them among the forged dies being used by Apolonio Guevara in Mexico City in the 1930s (App. II, Fig. 96-A). The presence of a *Mundos y Mares* with a forged assayer's mark automatically meant to Anderson that it too was a forgery.

The evidence, however, of these undeniably genuine dated candlesticks proves that the marks "LIN" over "CR," a *Mundos y Mares* and an eagle were being used by a silversmith (or shop) in 1729. This would indicate that the other marks illustrated by Anderson (App. II, Fig. 86, and Fig. 87, No. 8-F) are forgeries of these earlier stamps, rather than those of Lince González.

Of the ecclesiastic silver from South America, five pieces are from Paraguay, where the Jesuits exerted a powerful influence. They were transmitters of the flamboyant style of baroque Rome, the site of their mother church, Il Gesú, one of the most influential examples of church architecture in the western world. It embodies the spirit of the Counter-Reformation, of which the Society of Jesus, founded in Spain in 1534 by Ignatius Loyola, was one of the most effective arms in the fight against the Protestant Reformation.

One means used by the Jesuits to promote the Catholic position was to proclaim the wealth, grandeur and power of the Roman Church through this ornate art style—sometimes with eye-staggering results. Baroque art, and its less virile descendent, the rococo, became the orthodox style of church ornament everywhere in the Catholic world. Some remote areas, such as the southwestern part of the United States, were affected only slightly, but Mexico, Central and South America adopted them without reservation and translated them into local architectural and decorative styles which are among the most flamboyant in the world.

A pair of baroque candlesticks from the I.B.M. Collection (Fig. 7), with their intricate repoussé designs, would have fitted perfectly into any of the city churches built by *La Compañía de Jesús* (The Society of Jesus) in South America. They typify the restless, never-ending movement of the high baroque style. Swelling contours and flower motifs seem to move upward along the stems to break into flamelike designs around the bottoms of their hollow candle-bases. One base is collapsed, causing that candlestick to be three and a half centimeters shorter than the other. Each piece is composed of five parts on a central rod: base, lower stem, upper stem, candle-base and *bobêche*. Although they are two and a half centimeters taller (undamaged) each weighs 2.44 kg., about three pounds less than the ones from Mexico (Fig. 6), which weigh 3.777 kg. and 3.904 kg., (8 pounds 5¼ ounces and 8 pounds 9¾ ounces).

A chain of rural missions established by the Jesuits in Paraguay in 1610 was noted for its decorative architectural style. Metal work executed by Indians under their direction reflected this in a blending of elaborate European motifs and native interpretations. These objects, an increasingly rare Spanish Colonial style, are not only more complicated but are also crafted with more expertise than is usual in mission work. When the Jesuits were expelled from all Spanish dominions in 1767, the Paraguayan missions were abandoned and their ruins are now disintegrating in the jungle. Silver objects made to furnish or decorate them were scattered so, as E. Boyd says, "We are fortunate in having these examples [Figs. 8 & 9] of the style as expressed by indigenous silversmiths of the period, since many such pieces were melted down later on to be reshaped in more modern forms."[5]

One, a hammered and repoussé candelabrum (Fig. 8) combines two forms: a three standard candle-holder and a three-quarter nimbus of the type called a *resplandor* (splendor, radiance) which, in an inverted position, was usually attached to the head of a statue of the Virgin. The difference in the quality of workmanship between the central stem of the candelabrum and the *resplandor* suggests that this too may have been a nimbus for a statue which was added to an existing candlestick to convert it into a more impressive piece. Such concoctions were often improvised in frontier mission stations. Here the densely patterned nimbus, with leaping flames tipped with stars, serves as a reflector for three candles in fluted *bobêches*. The massive *resplandor* is supported on the back by a hand-wrought iron brace.

A half-circle *resplandor* for a statue of the Virgin (Fig. 4), found about twenty years ago in a cave in the desert country of Socorro County, is owned by L. D. Lupton of Silver City, New Mexico. It was probably part of a cache hidden by Apaches after a raid against one of the Jesuit missions in Sonora prior to 1767. When Governor Juan Bautista de Anza sent out a military detachment in 1780 to scout this area for a new road between Santa Fe and Sonora, it found such a cave which "literally was full of booty which had been stolen from time to time by the Apaches and stored here for future needs."[6]

The back view (bottom) illustrates one repoussé technique: pressing a thin sheet of metal from the back and then tooling it until the design is formed. This *resplandor*, which probably came from Mexico, is neither as densely decorated nor as expertly crafted as the one on the candelabrum from Paraguay.

Taullard, in his *Platería sudamericana*, describes a winged cherub wearing a *bobêche* for a crown very like the seventeenth century pair from Paraguay (Fig. 9).[7] Each is composed of three parts fastened to a steel back support. The heads, which are large in proportion and much heavier than the bodies, were cast in molds and soldered into place. Details on the wings and bodies are hand-tooled repoussé; some on the eyes and hair are chiseled. The beaded saucers and candle-holders were made separately, then fastened to the tops of the heads on a stem.

A magnificent baptismal shell (Fig. 10) collected by agents of I.B.M. Corporation in Peru, combines all of the decorating techniques commonly used by Spanish Colonial silversmiths except chasing: tooling, repoussé, die-stamping, casting, appliqué and chiseling. Fonts such as this were used in the homes of wealthy Spanish colonials, which often contained private chapels. This is a particularly fine example in form, style and technique.

The design is a typical shell form with a convex semicircle on the back which modulates gently into a shallow trough for water. The whole

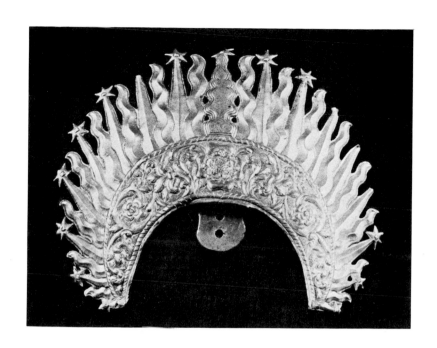

NIMBUS found near Socorro, New Mexico (front and back views)

Figure 4

convex section is precisely tooled in a repoussé design around a shield of Castile, León and Granada, supported on either side by rampant lions in a swirl of foliage. A crown above the shield is composed of delicate appliqué flowers which are also scattered among the leaf motifs. A raised edge, chiseled into tiny tripartite sections, borders the design area. Sixteen fluted ribs with die-stamped edges flare outward to an applied border of cast dentilation. Taullard, who shows a similar shell, dates this style in the late eighteenth century.[8]

Altogether, there are six silver crowns for images of Christ and the Virgin in the five collections. Such crowns, made everywhere in Latin America, vary from life-size to miniature. Both extremes are illustrated in two examples from Guatemala (Fig. 11-A & B*). The larger weighs 233.89 gr. (8¼ ounces) and the smaller 7.09 gr. (a quarter of an ounce). The miniature, only two centimeters in diameter, (about three-quarters of an inch), is silver filigree, a technique in which many colonial silver-smiths excelled. Some filigree work was done almost everywhere, but it is not as typical of the decorative style of Guatemala as the larger crown, which is hammered and tooled in a two-dimensional relief design composed of cut-out flower, bud and leaf motifs. Gem sets, which origi-nally held colored stones, are now empty. Its slightly bent headband was made separately and attached with solder.

An eighteenth century crown from Colombia (Fig. 12-A) represents the rich decorative style of colonial church interiors in Bogotá and Tunja. Typically, Colombian church ornament, though dense, is defined by frames, moldings or borders. A covered sugar bowl (not illustrated) which Mrs. Lyman bought in Colombia, exhibits these same characteristics. It, like the crown, is completely covered with tooled, stamped and chiseled carpet-like patterns arranged in areas separated by borders.

All of the ten Colombian pieces in these collections have a distinctive look which is easily recognized but difficult to describe. This is not entirely a matter of decoration, for most of the domestic articles are severely plain. It has, rather, to do with the quality and feel of the silver itself. There is a faint yellowish sheen and a surface hardness which suggest that the metal might be an amalgam. If true, this would account for the lightness and thinness of these objects compared to those from other areas. This crown, though almost twelve and a half centimeters (almost 5 inches) tall, with a disproportionately large finial, weighs only 141.75 gr. (5 ounces). This distinction is easily recognized when its exposed edges are compared to those on the large Guatemalan crown (Fig. 11-A).

A tiny nimbus (Fig. 12-B) is the only example from Ecuador. It was originally attached to the back of the head of a small *santo* (figure of a saint) by a long pin which protruded forward from a center medallion. Fashioned from rather heavy silver wire which has been cut and soldered, it is tooled into a decorative openwork design surrounded by sharply cut silver rays.

During the second half of the eighteenth century the baroque and rococo styles were outmoded in Europe by a strong reaction, a desire to return to the simple forms and uncluttered spaces of Renaissance art. The new style, variously called the "classical reaction" or the neoclassic, came to Mexico when the Royal Academy of San Carlos was established in 1785. The school's European masters, particularly Manuel Tolsá, were imbued with the spirit of classicism. The reaction did not, however, make itself felt in the silversmith's art until a new generation of apprentices had been trained at the academy.[9] Even then, the neoclassic style made little impression in Mexico and South America; Spanish colonials loved florid forms too much to give them up. It might, however, have had greater impact if the Latin American wars of liberation had not interrupted its development. By the time the revolutionary wars were over the romantic movement had swept across Europe, and Latin America again returned to a decorative art style, this time tempered by the plush daintiness of Victorianism.

There are only three neoclassic ecclesiastic objects in the collections: an incense boat, a chrismatory (container for holy oils) and a small tray which could have been used for an alms dish or to hold cruets for wine and water. The incense boat with attached spoon (Fig. 13-A) is one of the pieces collected by Miss M. V. Conkey in the 1930s. It was purchased originally by Bernardo Abeitia in Mexico between 1814 and 1816 when he made a special trip to buy furnishings for his private chapel, the Santuario de Esquipulas near Chimayo, New Mexico. Although the outside of the boat is smoothly planished, visible hammer marks on the inside reveal that it was made by the old hand hammered method. This consisted of shaping a thick sheet of metal by tapping it countless times with a small hammer. Planishing, or smoothing, was accomplished by further tapping with a small, flat mallet. Two precisely fitted lids are hinged on either side of a trough for the spoon when not in use. The handle of the spoon is thickened enough to hold a strong eyelet through which the first link of a double eyelet chain is passed. The boat, in excellent condition, stands on a short pedestal and base of classical style and proportions.

A chrismatory, sometimes called an *oleo,* was part of the personal equipment of every priest. He carried it with him to perform duties away from the sanctuary such as baptising newborn babies who might not live, blessing the ill, or performing the last rites for the dying. It contained the holy oils required for these services, each in its own section. The one illustrated (Fig. 13-B) was probably part of the furnishings imported from France by Archbishop Lamy after he came to Santa Fe in 1851. The engraved lettering which identifies each section is quite different stylistically from that on Spanish Colonial pieces. It is stamped with a tiny mark (too faint to photograph) which is the right size and shape to be a head of Hermes, a mark required on all French exports after 1879.[10] Another chrismatory from Spain (not illustrated) is almost identical, except that it has only two sections: the *Sanctum Chrisma* and the *Oleo Infirma*.

If the mark described above is actually a head of Hermes, then this chrismatory belongs properly outside the colonial period. However, according to E. Boyd, though New Mexico became a territory of the United States in 1851, it was not until the railroads came in the late 1870s and early 1880s that the material culture was appreciably changed and at least another ten years before it could be described as anything but Spanish Colonial. It was felt, therefore, that a few articles from the Territorial period should be included with the Spanish Colonial material.

The small alms tray (Fig. 14-A) is inscribed with *"ESTE PLATO LO MANDO HACER EL S. C. D. M. C. LEMUS EL MES D MAYO D 1837."* Translated this reads, "THIS PLATE WAS ORDERED MADE FOR THE SENOR CURA DON M. C. LEMUS IN THE MONTH OF MAY 1837." The date is followed by an indistinguishable die-stamp of what was probably an ecclesiastic insignia. It was collected by Mrs. Field who said in a note that she got it from Father Docher, a priest at Isleta Pueblo. It is smoothly planished and perfectly plain except for a simple tooled border of a type popular in Mexico since the seventeenth century.

A reliquary, properly defined, is a container for a sacred relic. In Roman Catholic churches they are often caskets of gold or silver, sometimes decorated with precious stones. A more general use of the term applies to anything which contains an object of sacred memory. The reliquary in the Museum of New Mexico Collection (Fig. 14-B) is in this category. It is a case for a bone carving of St. Joseph holding the Christ Child under a rather strange looking tree. A bearded saint, probably one of the Apostles, is carved on the reverse side. The images are enclosed in a silver frame between two pieces of glass now so worn that they obscure vision. The museum acquired the reliquary from Mauricio Sánchez of Albuquerque, who said that it came from the maternal side of his family.

Analysis of the foregoing material shows that, in spite of the limited number of ecclesiastic pieces in the five collections, they are widely distributed in time, place, type and style. Thus they provide a good selection for comparison with the five provincial articles from New Mexico discussed in Chapter VI of this study.

FOOTNOTES

[1]Cleve Hallenbeck, *Land of the Conquistadores* (Caldwell, Idaho: The Caxton Printers, Ltd., 1950), pp. 284–286.

[2]Richard E. Ahlborn, *The Ecclesiastic Silver of Colonial Mexico* (1968 Winterthur Conference Report. Winterthur, Delaware: Henry Francis du Pont Museum, 1969), pp. 27–28.

[3]Lawrence Anderson, *The Art of the Silversmith in Mexico 1519–1936,* Vol. I (New York: Oxford University Press, 1941), pp. 309–310.

[4]Ibid., p. 303.

[5]E. Boyd, "Colonial Silver from Latin America," *El Palacio,* Vol. 69/2 (1962), p. 119.

[6]Hallenbeck, p. 241.

[7]Alfredo Taullard, *Platería sudamericana* (Buenos Aires: Peuser, Ltda., 1941), Fig. 147.

[8]Ibid., Fig. 162.

[9]Anderson, Vol. I, p. 231.

[10]Seymour B. Wyler, *The Book of Old Silver* (New York: Crown Publishers, 1937), p. 380.

CHAPTER IV

DOMESTIC SILVER

What is it that attracts us so greatly, apart from antiquarian sentimentality, in these pre-industrial crafts like colonial silversmithing? When I mentally take inventory of things made in the colonial worlds of America, certain shared qualities begin to stand out. Among these the one I want to discuss today has to do with colonial surfaces.

The American colonial surface, whether it is of silver or adobe or clapboard or walnut or mahogany, can be called a strong surface, in the sense that the entire shell of the container or the instrument, is generously measured out from the marvelous abundance of raw materials in America. If the notion of a strong surface is difficult to imagine, please think of a poorly made flaking veneer or buckling plywood surface, and you have a weak surface. The strong surface is integral and no cleavages weaken its inner structure.

It is a real difference between mother country and colony that weak surfaces were actively sought after in Europe. Veneering for instance was new in 1664, but its American use remained unnecessary until long after. There is little marquetry in rural America. Sheffield plate, made by fusing silver on copper, was invented in England in 1742 but the American use of fusion did not appear until *much later*. The point is that material scarcities in Europe enforced the technical achievement of weak surfaces, whereas the abundance in America made weak surfaces less necessary.[1]

This long passage from George Kubler's opening address before the Fourteenth Annual Winterthur Conference in 1968 is quoted in full because it so eloquently describes the most characteristic constant of Spanish Colonial silver: a strong sense of surface, the result, in part, of excessive weight which reflects the abundance of raw materials in America. This intrinsic quality is more evident in domestic articles than in any other classification of colonial silver except provincial. Ecclesiastic objects, ornaments, accessories and gear are usually decorated—some excessively so. Although one is always conscious of their weight, surface decoration often minimizes the tactile qualities usually produced by so generous a use of silver. Domestic silver, which tends to be plain, exposes surfaces and thus heightens the effect of inherent characteristics.

The visual impact is considerable, especially upon people who have never seen Spanish Colonial silver. Their reaction is so consistent as to be predictable: "It *looks* like solid silver but it can't be, just *see* how heavy it is!" The notion that one can see quality and weight results partly from the method used in making these old pieces. Most Spanish Colonial plate was made, as mentioned earlier, by the technique of hammering or raising a sheet of thick, soft metal into the desired form with a mallet, then planishing it with a small flat-faced tool to erase indentations left by the hammer.[2]

Although surfaces thus achieved by expert silversmiths are remarkably smooth, this method produced a surface shimmer more often felt than seen. Less skilled artisans left visible hammer marks which actually emphasize the sense of surface. These small, uneven dents reflect the light, imparting an incomparably rich and eloquent texture. Rims and borders, such as beading, were sometimes made separately and applied to finished articles, but most edges, particularly on plates, were tooled into a variety of shapes and patterns. Accessory parts, such as feet, legs, standards, handles, spouts and finials, were often cast and attached with solder.

There is no clean-cut separation between domestic and ecclesiastic in Spanish Colonial silver. Objects such as candlesticks, candle snuffers, trays incense burners, pitchers, basins, frames, salt dishes, covered cups, platters, saucers and plates could be used interchangeably. Separation into categories for purposes of this study, therefore, is based upon probable use and historic reference. Some articles, discussed as domestic silver or accessories, could have been used equally in the church.

Most forms of Spanish Colonial silver were of European origin. The arts of Spain's colonies generally duplicated the stylistic development of the mother country with a time lag of twenty-five to fifty years. For example, a mid-nineteenth century helmet-shaped ewer (Fig. 15) in the Field Collection is almost the same shape as a jug from the third quarter of the eighteenth century illustrated in Stéphane Faniel's *French Art of the 18th. Century*.[3] Such sophisticated European styles became particularly popular in Mexico during the reign of Maximilian and Carlotta (1864–67). The ewer is stamped on the handle and base with the genuine marks of Chief Assayer Antonio del Castillo, who held office between January 21, 1861 and March 13, 1862 and again from June 1867 to February 1868.[4] Another stamp, which might be a silversmith's mark, is barely visible on the edge of the handle.

Pitchers like this were used in homes of wealthy colonials as bedroom appointments with large silver wash basins like one in the Morley Collection (Fig. 35-A). The ewer is the most elaborately decorated piece of Mexican domestic plate in the collections. A repoussé spray of naturalistic flowers and buds circles a pyriform (pear shaped) body on either side of an escutcheon with etched border. The same floral motif, inscribed beneath a wide rim, is balanced by a formal design around the base below a low plinth. A cast handle, composed of graceful leaf forms, describes a series of smooth flowing counter curves. Velvety smooth surfaces indicate the hand of a master and the surface shimmer described earlier is so rich that it can be detected in the photograph of the piece.

The presence of legal marks on Mexican silver does not necessarily mean that the object was made by a master. The name (or contraction thereof) required was that of the silver shop, not the individual artisan. Often the name of the master and the shop were the same and it is usually easy to recognize the work of the former. An article, however, stamped with a master's name may have been made by an employee, a partner or a member of the family.[5] When only one name is found on an object, it is usually that of the chief assayer, whose stamp was required by law after 1733. He may, or may not, have been the silversmith who made the article. In order to assign Mexican silver it is necessary to understand the purpose and system of marking during the colonial period.

Marking was better controlled in Mexico than in other parts of colonial Latin America. It was done for one reason only: to prevent tax evasion. This does not imply that fraud was not practiced elsewhere, but the absence of marks on most silver from South America indicates that their laws either were different or were not enforced so rigidly. It also suggests that the problem of fraudulent practices may not have been as critical there as in Mexico, where the tax on mined silver was twenty per cent plus one and a half per cent for smelting and assaying and an additional tax of three *reales* for each *marco* on silver used in coins.[6]

Such heavy taxes could never be made effective, and those concerned took the only course that permitted them to live: fraud. The miners presented a part of the silver for coinage and paid the corresponding tax; but on that sold for commercial purposes as well as that to be fabricated into plate and jewelry, a great part paid no taxes. This was one of the principal reasons for the great quantities of jewelry and plate found in Mexican homes. Nearly a fourth part of the value of the metal was thus saved and it was converted into objects readily saleable in emergencies.[7]

It is easy to see that owning silver plate was not entirely a matter of status, though certainly that was an important consideration in colonial society. It was also an excellent investment. An individual who bought silver on which no tax had been paid was not only able to sell it profitably but could also have it converted into coins in time of need.

The problem of illegal fabrication of silver in Mexico plagued the crown from earliest times. According to José Torre Revello, eight licensed *plateros* came to the New World before 1516. The first was a master silversmith, Pablo Belvis, whose name is listed with several officials who went to the Island of Española in 1495.[8] Evidently many came during the first years after the conquest because, by 1526, Charles V and Queen Juana felt compelled to issue a *cédula* (decree) forbidding either gold- or silversmiths to work in Mexico because "it had come to their attention that some had been defrauding the crown."[9]

The situation was somewhat regularized by 1559, when the prohibition was finally revoked and permission to work was granted. Meanwhile, a silversmith's guild, which was to become the model for others throughout Spanish America, had been organized in Mexico City and a system of inspections established. In 1532 an act of the *cabildo* (municipal council) of Mexico City decreed that *veedores* (inspectors) were to be selected from the membership of the guild and made responsible for compliance with the law.

The absence of a silversmith's mark on a piece of Mexican colonial silver in no way decreases its value. Regulations requiring a silversmith's (or shop's) mark were never fully complied with, probably because, once an article had been assayed and taxed, authorities considered the stamping of the artisan's name no longer essential.[10] After 1733, chief assayer's marks are the key to dating, to within the time he held office. If a silversmith's dates coincide with those of a chief assayer, and both marks are found on an object, it is sometimes possible to date it by the artisan's name as recorded in the guild's membership rolls.[11]

It should be clear from the foregoing evidence that much genuine Spanish Colonial silver is not marked at all. There are 130 pieces in the present collections with marks and 199 without. Any large collection which includes items from both North and South America would probably conform very nearly to this same ratio.

Tea and coffee services did not become part of the silversmith's repertoire of forms until late in the seventeenth century. The earliest silver teapot in England was made in 1670 and the first coffee pot in 1681. Tea was at first believed to be a beneficial medicine and coffee a drug so dangerous to health that several attempts were made to introduce bills into Parliament to prohibit its sale.[12]

In spite of this, both drinks soon became popular and led, in the eighteenth century, to the fabrication of some of the most common articles of modern tableware: tea and coffee pots, cups with saucers, teaspoons (reduced copies of the tablespoons then in use), covered sugar bowls, milk and cream pitchers and specialty items such as tea caddies (canisters), hot water pots and warming racks.[13]

Three examples from the Morley Collection are variations of the pyriform shape, one of the most popular of eighteenth century forms. The coffee pot (Fig. 16-A*) was made in Mexico within twenty-two years after she won her independence from Spain. It is clearly stamped with the genuine marks of Chief Assayer Cayetano Buitrón (1823-1843), the first to replace the crown of Spain over the "M" with the small "o" of Mexico. There is no silversmith's mark. The body of the pot is a true pear shape with a large, simply carved wooden handle opposite the spout. Some coffee and teapots had straight handles set at right angles to the spout, but this was not too successful with heavy vessels which required a firm grip. It stands on a simple pedestal which prevents the hot container from marring tables or other surfaces. A wide domed lid fits well down over the rim to retain heat within the vessel. The whole is impressively plain and massive.

Both the milk pitcher and the teapot (Fig. 16-B* & C*) are eighteenth century pieces from Guatemala which, with the rest of Central America, was part of the Viceroyalty of New Spain during the colonial period. The city of Santiago de los Caballeros de Goathemala was founded by the *conquistador* Don Pedro de Alvarado in 1524. It was moved twice before 1541, at which time the capital was officially established in the shadow of three giant volcanoes in the highlands of Guatemala: *Agua* (Water), *Fuego* (Fire) and their companion, *Acatenango*. The city was renamed Antigua when the seat of government was moved to the present site of Guatemala City after the former was almost completely destroyed by a cataclysmic eruption and earthquake on July 29, 1773.[14]

These peaks are particularly important in relation to colonial silver because several depictions of them were used on Guatemala-Chiapas marks. The most common one shows Santiago (St. James Major, the patron saint of Spain) on horseback flying over two peaks. On others there are three peaks and sometimes only one. More rarely, a lion replaces Santiago, or an "S S" *(Señor Santiago)* flanks either side of one peak. Usually, but not always, these stamps are accompanied by one of several small, delicate crowns. Evidently both marks, together or separately, signified that the *quinto* had been paid and that the metal was of the required standard. Some pieces were stamped with only the crown and others with only the Santiago.

We know that silversmiths worked in Antigua soon after the city was founded because *plateros* are mentioned in records of the *Cabildo* between 1524 and 1530. An account of one case of fraud before the *Ayuntamiento* (City Council) of Guatemala in 1540 resulted in a ruling which required that all silversmiths post bond, indicating that the crown had the same trouble there as in Mexico.[15]

The silversmith's guild of Guatemala was not established until 1745, over two hundred years after its model in Mexico City. Prior to that time artisans were evidently responsible to the *Ayuntamiento* for, among numerous references relating to *plateros,* one in particular says, "In September of 1726 the master gold and silversmith Antonio de Lima presented a petition to the *Ayuntamiento* asking that it enforce the silversmith's ordinances of Mexico City."[16]

The small, eighteenth century milk or cream pitcher (Fig. 16-B*) is stamped with a crown and Santiago over three peaks. The teapot (Fig. 16-C*), which Dr. Morley found in Campeche, has a different crown and Santiago over two peaks. Both are pyriform shapes, but the bulge on the teapot is low and flattened against a large base. This type was often placed on a silver stand or rack to raise the hot vessel off damageable surfaces. It is perfectly plain except for a pineapple finial on a hinged lid which is fastened to a metal element supporting the top of an impressive wooden handle. Domed lids such as this were usually deeper on teapots than on coffee pots because it was believed such depth improved the steeping process of the beverage. It is stamped with a monogram composed of the letters "RNB," probably an owner's initials rather than a silversmith's mark because regulations required that the latter use either their full names or a recognizable contraction of them. It was not, however, unusual for owners to have silver plate stamped with their names (examples: App. II, Fig. 97-A). These were usually placed opposite, or otherwise separated from, official marks. Monograms, however, were customarily engraved, not die-stamped, so this mark is somewhat of an enigma.

Although many of the candlesticks in the collections would have been as appropriate for colonial churches or chapels as for homes, the suitability of such use for a Peruvian candelabrum (Fig. 17) is questionable because it expresses nationalistic rather than religious sentiments. It represents a style revival of the early Republican period (c. 1820–c.1860) in which a deliberate attempt was made to popularize indigenous colonial styles. The *Mestizo* was a distinctive eighteenth century Peruvian style which resulted from a fusing of European forms with local influences. It had added new and exotic motifs in which strange New World varieties replaced the familiar flowers, vines, leaves, animals and human forms from which intricately intertwined Mannerist decorations were constructed. Separately cast or stamped ornamental details were both applied and assembled to create dense, lacy patterns of positive and negative spaces quite different from other stylistic variations of Spanish Colonial silver. In the Republican revival of the style, native motifs which pointed to Peruvian history not related to Spain, such as the figure of the "noble Inca" which supports the triple standard of this candelabrum, were emphasized. These articles, sometimes called Independence pieces, often depict an Inca noble (symbolizing Peru) standing on a lion (symbolizing Spain) and surrounded by llamas, parrots, turkeys and foliage typical of the land.[17]

Only a few of the South American pieces in these collections are hallmarked. This does not mean that the *quinto* was not collected, nor that assayers, inspectors and silversmiths organizations did not exist. Guilds and Confraternities of San Eloy, the religious organization restricted to silversmiths and dedicated to their patron saint, were organized throughout colonial Spanish America.

People sometimes facetiously observe that one reason Peruvian articles were not stamped may have been because silver was so plentiful that it didn't matter whether the tax was collected—that colonials could use all they wanted and still send so much wealth to Spain that they would not be questioned by the authorities. Of course this could be no more true in Peru than in Mexico, although both areas were incredibly rich in mineral wealth. In spite of the fantastic riches yielded to Spain, especially by Peru, the notion that her greedy monarchs would have permitted laxness in the collection of taxes is naive.

A much more reasonable explanation can be assumed from Emilio Harth-Terre's description of the early ordinances of Cuzco. They provided that an ". . . Indian overseer, who knew how to read and write Spanish,

44

also took part in appraising the work as to fine content and quality of workmanship. He accompanied the assayer in the casting and marking of the ingots and the payment of the Royal Fifth."[18] No doubt the only purpose of marking here (as in Mexico) was to prevent tax evasion and, since the *quinto* was collected when the ingots were made, there would be no reason for further stamping.

The richest mine in the New World was discovered at Cerro de Potosí in upper Peru (now Bolivia) in 1545. The town of Potosí, established as an imperial city by Charles V in 1546, had a population of from 120,000 to 160,000 by 1571. Its silversmith's guild was one of the wealthiest in Spanish America.[19] A *casa de moneda* (mint), built in 1572, collected the *quinto* for the crown. This must have amounted to a fantastic figure, for by the end of the seventeenth century, there were over three thousand mine entrances in this *cerro* (hill) alone.

Potosí was not the only silver producing area in the Peruvian highlands. There were over two hundred mines in full operation by the eighteenth century, from some of which chunks of pure silver weighing nearly four hundred pounds were taken. With such quantities of raw material available, it is not surprising that the artisans of Potosí, Cuzco, Lima and Ayacucho produced some of the greatest masterpieces of the silversmith's art in all Spanish America.[20]

One example of such artistry is an exquisite eighteenth century filigree tray made in Ayacucho (Fig. 21-A). It represents another typically Peruvian style which, though derived from Europe, was transformed in a manner described by Carlos Neuhaus Ugarteche, president of the Art Foundation of Peru and the Museum of Art of Lima:

The *plateresque* style which began in Spain at the beginning of the 16th. century with the work of the German silversmith, Enrique de Arfe, arrived in Peru a century later but took on a more agile and lighter mode of expression.

This differentiation with respect to the Spanish *plateresque* style is most noticeable in the so-called "silver filigree" work done in Huamanga (now Ayacucho) during the 18th. century. Such marvelous work was no longer just filigree but rather true silver lace, the product of a native style created in Peru. Neither the silver worked in Spain or England, nor that of the Italian Renaissance or French rococo possessed such exquisite and elegant lightness as did the native filigree work, or silver lacework, of Ayacucho. It was different from the work done with the gold "threads" of Toledo, different from the silver filament work which arrived from Damascus. It had characteristics which were different from those objects coming from the Philippines or China. It may be justly affirmed that such work was native to Peru.[21]

One distinction between Ayacucho filigree and that from other parts of the world is a matter of weight. This delicate tray, only 32 cm. (18 inches) long, looks as light as air; yet it weighs 574.09 gr. (1 pound 4¼ ounces). A feathery design is spread so densely over a basal rim and frame that the tray is as strong as a piece of plain heavy plate. Thread-like ribs with smooth leaf terminals intersect a delicate petal rim outlined with a thin silver rope.

Architectural details were important design elements for Renaissance and post-Renaissance silversmiths. The four pairs of candlesticks illustrated represent several in the collections which derive from various balustrade designs. Two pairs (Figs. 18 & 19-B*), collected by Dr. and Mrs. Morley in Guatemala, are seventeenth century and bear the same hallmarks: a lion facing left over two peaks and a crown. The shorter pair (Fig. 19-B) is stamped with an additional crown surmounted by a cross, indicating that they may have been made for an ecclesiastic.

When received by the museum they were smoke blackened as if they had survived a fire. This would have been probable if they had been made in Antigua, still the capital of Guatemala in the seventeenth century. Comparison between these and a shorter but broader similar baluster candlestick from Spain (Fig. 20) points up a major difference between European and Spanish Colonial silver. Those from Guatemala (Fig. 19-B) weigh over 737.1 gr. (1 pound 10 ounces) each, while the one from Spain weighs only seven ounces. They have the same textured surface but the latter lacks the deep, rich patina which results from excessive weight.

A pair of baroque candlesticks from Austria (Fig. 19-A*) might not properly belong in a collection of Spanish Colonial silver except that they represent the short reign of Maximilian and Carlotta in Mexico. Each is stamped with a large "M" (surmounted by a crown) with Carlotta's name on one side and that of a silversmith named "V. FUSTER" on the other. Another object from the same period (not illustrated) is decorated with rococo elegance. It is a small bedside tumbler inset with five large coins, identified by George C. Miles, chief curator of the American Numismatic Society, as a two-mark piece of Charles XII of Sweden, dated 1701, and four half-thalers from the reign of Frederick the Great of Prussia, dated 1750. Like the candlesticks, the tumbler represents the florid styles so favored by Germanic peoples in the nineteenth century.

Platters and trays of all kinds were widely used by Spanish colonials.

Some, like an oblong platter (Fig. 21-B*) from Mexico which is stamped with an owner's mark "ROZAS" in addition to those of Chief Assayer Antonio Forcada y La Plaza (1791-1818), and a fish platter (Fig. 23-B) which Mrs. Lyman bought in Colombia, were deep enough to serve as vegetable bowls. The narrow applied border on the fish platter is decorated with hundreds of tiny silver filets, each attached separately. It is stamped on the rim with an unidentified mark.

Two comparisons illustrate the metallic distinctions between Colombian and other colonial silver noted earlier in relationship to the small Colombian crown. One is between this fish platter and a Guatemalan example illustrated on the same page (Fig. 23-A). These two pieces, photographed under exactly the same conditions, both have large plain surfaces which reveal subtle differences in color and texture. The metal in the Colombian piece is thinner and also feels and looks harder, suggesting an amalgam. This impression is supported by the fact that its sides were raised to a height of 4½ cm. (1¾ inches) without flutes, ribs or other devices to support its weight. Although its superficial area is about twice that of the Guatemalan piece, it weighs only about a third more. The smaller platter, which is stamped with yet another variation of the Guatemalan hallmark (this time with a rather playful lion leaping to the right over three peaks) presents an almost blue-white velvety surface. It is raised gradually from the bowl to a height of only 2 cm. (less than an inch) and then its weight is counterbalanced by a wide convex rim and thumb print border.

These differences are even more clearly revealed by the second comparison, in which the weight relationship is reversed. A footed salver from Mexico (Fig. 26-A) is only about a third larger than a scalloped plate from Colombia (Fig. 26-B), yet it weighs over twice as much. Here the softly modulated surface of the Mexican piece contrasts sharply with the crisp texture of the Colombian plate. Also, short cast feet are strategically placed to reinforce its pinched flutes in order to support the weight of soft metal. It is stamped with a single mark, an eagle in a square, unlike any used by chief assayers during the eighteenth and early nineteenth centuries, so it was probably forged later to make the piece more saleable. A barely legible name, "Dn . . . ia Morales" has been deliberately erased and another, "Dn Ramon Solis" scratched on the botton rim.

Forged marks do not always mean that a piece is a reproduction. Early in the twentieth century dealers in Mexico and South America began to realize that the absence of marks on genuine old pieces hindered their sale to a public just becoming knowledgeable concerning the value of antiques. Consequently, they stamped many objects which had been unmarked originally with false marks, often using old punches saved from colonial times. Verification of colonial plate must, therefore, be based on stylistic analysis as well as hallmarks.

Some reproductions are marked as such with stamps used in Mexico after June 15, 1895, when the law was changed to make marking voluntary. If a silversmith desired he could present an object for testing and stamping by the assayer, but was not required to do so by law. A piece so marked was stamped with a number indicating the content of pure silver in thousandths. Sometimes, but not always, this number was preceded by the letter "L" (standing for *Ley*, standard) and/or the eagle used as a tax mark after the Revolution (App. II, Fig. 95, No. 23).

Such is the case with an excellent reproduction of a popular eighteenth century colonial style (Fig. 22-B*). A lobed platter with beaded rim, it is stamped with "800." Even without this mark, however, it would not have been difficult to spot this as a copy. One of the significant visual differences between reproductions and genuine colonial pieces results from lowered content of silver. From the time of the discovery of the Indies until June 9, 1728, the standard for silver in Mexico was eleven *dineros* and four grains out of twelve *dineros* (pure). After that, until Mexico's independence it was eleven *dineros* out of twelve.[22] Objects made after the colonial period do not have the glowing patina, partly due to age and wear, partly to weight and partly to silver content, which is consistently characteristic of older plate.

Reproductions of Spanish Colonial designs are now being mass produced throughout Latin America. Many are excellent, but if the purchaser wants an antique he should examine carefully for patina, color, weight, method of manufacture and evidence of wear. This is not to fault many modern silversmiths whose handmade objects are collectors' items. Silver plate made by mechanical methods, however, is not usually hard for the discerning eye to detect for, as Carlos Pizano y Saucedo says in *Plateria, siglo XX:*

In general, the outstanding evolution of the industry has gone parallel to a serious decrease in the authentic, natural and artistic value of the pieces. . . . Perfection, aesthetic value, technical quality and well balanced plastic solutions, have all been sacrificed in the benefit of comfort, speed, production volume and economy. . . . Plate rollers, dies and presses, precision tools and foundry equipment have decisively contributed to enrich the silversmith technology; but, simultaneously they have led to mass production.[23]

Although all old silver shows evidence of wear, much is not as marred as Dr. Morley's four-lobed platter (Fig. 22-A). It may have been produced in the shop of José María Rodallega, one of Mexico's great masters, whose last work was completed in 1807, but who, at seventy years of age, was still managing his silver shop in Mexico City in 1811. Though his most important pieces were ecclesiastic, he did many fine articles for domestic use. Anderson gives ''RGA,'' ''ROGA'' and ''RODA'' over ''LLEGA'' as his authentic marks.[24] This platter is stamped with ''RGDA'' and the genuine marks of Chief Assayer Forcada y La Plaza (App. II, Fig. 89, No. 10, with tax mark in No. 11).

This was probably the mark of Rodallega's shop which he continued to operate between 1807 and 1811, though he no longer worked himself. It seems more likely that an artist of his standing would have used a stamp with a different contraction of his name at that time to indicate that articles produced were not actually his own work. The fact that it appears with genuine assayer's marks automatically authenticates it, and no other silversmith is listed during Forcada's term (1791–1818) whose name can be contracted to these four letters.[25] A five-lobed plate in the Field Collection is stamped with this same set of marks. It is as simply designed except for a beautifully tooled concave-convex border (like Fig. 30-A). Both objects were obviously made by an expert craftsman.

A round tray (Fig. 24-A) and an oblong platter which, because of similarity is not illustrated, were made by the same Argentine silversmith. Both are stamped with ''LANO'' and the number ''900.'' The former could have been the name of either an assayer or a silversmith. We can recognize the artist's distinctive repoussé style in both articles. He chose a *chispa,* a small piece of shaped iron against which flint was struck to make fire, for his basic design element.

Chispas were used everywhere in the Spanish world during the colonial period. They varied in shape according to locale, but all consisted of a loop of metal with hooked ends turned inward. Those in New Mexico were shaped like an inverted ''U.'' In most places they were flattened, as in those depicted on the borders of these pieces. They are used horizontally on the tray to form the inside edge of a scalloped border. On the platter they are placed back-to-back in the shape of fleur-de-lys to completely cover the border.

The number ''900'' may have indicated, as in Mexico, the content of pure silver in thousandths and would have been stamped by an assayer. It could not have had the same significance as regards dating. In Mexico marks with numbers were not used until after 1895. This evidently was not true in Argentina because one of the pairs of stirrups (Fig. 54-A), stamped with the same "900," is almost exactly like one Taullard illustrates with a group of colonial styles.[26]

Alike except in size are three six-lobed round serving trays with molded cyma (convex-concave) borders and upright cast handles (Fig. 27-A). One bears rather obvious forgeries of Forcada's marks but, since it seems to be an old piece, was probably one of those articles stamped early in the twentieth century to make it more appealing to antique collectors. The other two are stamped with the genuine namemark of Chief Assayer Diego González de la Cueva, who held office between 1733 and 1788 (Fig. 82, No. 5). Two other marks shown with it on the tray illustrated are not authenticated by Anderson. There was, however, enough confusion concerning the use of eagle and crown stamps during González' term to cause his successor, José Antonio Lince González, to draw up new ordinances because "at this time there was apparently much fraud, and some confusion in regard to the stamp pertaining to the payment of the Royal Fifth."[27] These marks are so badly worn that it seems impossible they could have been stamped later than González' time. One unidentified mark, a strange backward "Z" with an "O" drawn through the diagonal, might be read as an "N" except that, any way you look at it, it is still backward.

A late seventeenth century finger bowl from Spain (Fig. 25-A), given to the Museum of New Mexico by Victor Hammer of New York, is actually a large shallow plate in which everyone rinsed his fingers as it was passed from person to person at table. Though of comparable size, it is dramatically lighter than the smallest of the Mexican trays just discussed. This, at 1.25 kg. (2 pounds 12 ounces), far outweighs the Spanish piece at 297.68 gr. (10½ ounces). The finger bowl is completely covered with late baroque repoussé decorations. Scroll and leaf designs alternate with diapered panels around a central medallion enclosed within a floral border and a tiny fluted edge. It is stamped with three indistinguishable marks and a monogram composed of a large "M" with a small "o" and "z," which probably stood for "Muñoz."

Sixty plates described here vary from small salad to large dinner size. One example of each of the seven designs represented is illustrated. Plain plates (Fig. 30-B) or lobed styles with plain edges (Fig. 27-B) were made throughout the colonial period, but in the eighteenth century variations of cyma borders became popular and lobes more complex. Earlier shapes were usually restricted to five or six simple lobes (Fig. 31-A). Neither these nor plain edges were dropped in the eighteenth century but new bordered shapes were added, varying from five to eight lobes (Fig. 28-B*) or even complex scallops (Fig. 26-B). Some were beaded (Fig. 24-B) or otherwise decorated (Fig. 29-B*).

Of the sixty plates studied, thirteen are unmarked and thus could be sixteenth or seventeenth century examples. The rest, except for one from Colombia, are stamped with either eighteenth or nineteenth century Mexican or Guatemalan marks. Some have owner's marks like the "CHABES" on the top rim of a six-lobed example (Fig. 31-A) which also has official stamps and a silversmith's mark on the bottom. Sometimes this was reversed, as on a plain plate (Fig. 30-B*), where legal marks are on the top and the owner's, "SAUTO," is on the bottom.

Many plates have *buriladas* (Fig. 42-B). These are Mexican marks which often puzzle collectors. They are zigzags, some large and some small, made by the burin when the assayer took a small amount of metal from an article to test for standard of quality. Officials were instructed not to mar the silver, so most *buriladas* are on the bottoms, but some are still definitely defacing. The sample for testing usually was taken at the time of hallmarking, so a *burilada* is good corroborative evidence concerning the genuineness of an article, but this is not invariably true. Some Mexican articles with full sets of marks do not have *buriladas* and some modern silversmiths imitate them in an attempt to foist off reproductions as genuine.[28]

Another Mexican mark should be described, although it was not found on any objects in the collections. It is an "R" crowned (App. II, Fig. 97-B), a die stamped on silver at the smelter as proof that the tax had been paid. It was sometimes stamped again on fabricated articles to prevent the tax from being collected a second time. Neither a hallmark nor a tax stamp, it is of little value in identifying or dating.[29]

Marks on plates illustrated represent the whole selection except for two unusual ones from Guatemala. One is a double "S" (Señor Santiago) on either side of one peak (Fig. 29-B*) and the other is a namemark surmounted by a crown (Fig. 24-B). The latter is probably the stamp of Captain Felipe Rivas de Angulo, chief assayer to the Marquis de Cadereyta, Viceroy of Mexico in 1724.[30] This must have been a private post because Rivas de Angulo was not a chief assayer in Mexico during the early eighteenth century.[31] It is unusual to find an assayer's or a silversmith's mark with the crown of Guatemala.

Domestic silver impressed North American visitors in Guatemala-Chiapas as much as it did early travelers to New Mexico. It was mentioned in particular by John Lloyd Stephens, a New York lawyer who aroused the interest of America in the Maya ruins of Central America when he wrote about his travels with an artist friend, Frederick Catherwood, in 1841. One incident occurred as they traveled on muleback across the mountains from Guatemala City to the ruins of Palenque in northern Chiapas: "The first afternoon we stopped at the hacienda of Sotaná [Chiapas]. . . . The next day, at the abode of Padre Solis, a rich old cura short and broad, living on a fine hacienda, we dined off solid silver dishes, drank out of silver cups, and washed in a silver basin.''[32]

Generally speaking, Guatemalan plate was more decorative than that of colonial Mexico. A fluted bowl with intricate cast handles (Fig. 31-B) exemplifies the type of etched floral motifs often used on silver knives, forks and spoons (Fig. 52-A). On the bowl, alternately wide and narrow convex-concave flutes end in a crenate edge below a broad, delicately engraved border which shows on both inside and outside. Tiny squirrels cling to handles composed of intertwined twigs with sprouting buds and leaves.

This piece is not marked, but is very like a Guatemalan bowl illustrated by Valle-Arizpe in *Arte y plata* of October, 1945.[33] The Philadelphia Museum of Art has another small bowl of the same style from Oaxaca in southern Mexico which they date between 1700 and 1800.[34] There was probably a good deal of style overlapping and exchange of articles between the southern states of Mexico and Guatemala, making it reasonable to suggest that a similar bowl (Fig. 35-B) with unusual marks—an eagle, a Guatemalan crown and ''Ramirez'' (unidentified)—may have been stamped by the *Caja Real* (royal treasury office) in Oaxaca.

By the end of the eighteenth century *Cajas Reales* had been established in provincial cities all over New Spain except in the far north.[35] In each an official was authorized to collect the tax, test the metal and affix marks. In southern Mexico there were *Cajas Reales* in Oaxaca, Campeche and Mérida, any of which could have used this set of marks. It should be remembered, however, that the teapot collected by Dr. Morley in Campeche (Fig. 16-C) is stamped with Guatemalan marks, a crown and Santiago over one peak, but does not include the eagle commonly used in Mexico.

One plain Mexican bowl (Fig. 35-B*) has a completely different visual impact from its decorated Guatemalan counterpart (Fig. 31-B). In the former the flutes were uniformly spaced and so rounded that they are actually lobes. This, plus the fact that its cast handles describe simple curves instead of complex lacy patterns, tends to create a feeling of monumentality lacking in the Guatemalan piece. This stylistic difference holds generally between Mexican and Guatemalan colonial plate.

Fluting and lobing served two purposes in the fabrication of bowls: to decorate and to strengthen the sides so they could be raised to bowl height. Two large bowls from Mexico (Fig. 32-A & 35-A*) and a tureen from Bolivia (Fig. 34-A) demonstrate this combining of decorative and structural elements. The smaller of the two Mexican bowls (Fig. 32-A) is the one Mrs. Field found in a chicken yard in Peña Blanca. Here, thirty flutes ascend without interruption through a change of angle to flare outward, terminating in a wide border with simple molded rim. It is stamped with the genuine marks of Chief Assayer Antonio Forcada y La Plaza (App. II, Fig. 89, No. 11), who held office between 1791 and 1818, and master silversmith Antonio Caamaño, *veedor* in Mexico City in 1799 and 1801.[36]

The larger bowl (Fig. 35-A), actually a wash basin, bears the most common of all authentic marks found on old Mexican plate, those of Cayetano Buitrón (App. II. Fig. 92, No. 16), chief assayer for the first twenty years of Mexican independence (1823-1843). At 38.1 cm., (about 15 inches) in diameter, the bowl weighs 1.7 kg. (3¾ pounds). In order to support this excessive weight, thirty-two flutes are raised almost vertically with a narrow tooled edge before angling to the border. The bottom (on the inside) is decorated with a chased floral spray around the monogram "F. B." in the center.

Although the Morleys acquired most of their silver in Guatemala, one of their most impressive bowls (Fig. 33-A*) is almost certainly an eighteenth century Mexican piece. In terms of style, its elegant simplicity is more typical of Mexico than Guatemala and its expert craftsmanship speaks of a skilled urban artist. No object in the collections exhibits more subtle surface modulations than those revealed by the broad expanse of this handsomely proportioned bowl. Large hand-wrought handles set beneath a firmly turned rim describe its total restraint. The name "Doña Maria Antonia Rocha" is amateurishly inscribed on the bottom.

Another indigenous colonial style revived in Peru early in Republican times (c. 1825-1900) is called "Andean." Much simpler than the *Mestizo* but, like it, incorporating motifs from Peru's ancient past, it used the images and plain surfaces of Inca art to express the spirit of the *altiplano*. A mid-nineteenth century sugar bowl (Fig. 33-B), collected by Miss Florence Dibell Bartlett, is a splendid example of this style. Small gold and silver figures with hands on their stomachs and llamas with pricked-up ears were so standardized in Inca art that they varied only in points of detail. Here they are used for feet, handles and finial on the lid. These llamas, especially the three saddled ones on the bottom, are more expressively active than their ancient prototypes, but the tiny handles are almost exact replicas of Inca figures.

Some forms of Spanish Colonial silver did not exist in areas of America colonized by the French or English. Notable among them are articles related to smoking. For example, *braserillos* (braziers), which were passed at table for guests to light cigars or cigarettes, and women's tobacco boxes called *tabaqueras,* were common in Spanish Colonial areas. It must have shocked early Anglo visitors in New Mexico to find women smoking.

An old illustration from George Wilkins Kendall's *Narrative of the Texan Santa Fe Expedition*, reproduced in *Matt Field on the Santa Fe Trail*, shows two girls smoking in the doorway of an adobe house. The caption reads, "Many of the Santa Fe señoritas smoked 'Chupars,' a thimble full of fine tobacco folded up in a bit of corn shucks."[37]

Two nineteenth century *braserillos* are illustrated (Fig. 32-B* & 36-A). Such small braziers consisted of trays, sometimes with handles, fastened to cups which held live coals. Both cups and trays varied in size, shape and ornament. Some were quite elegant, but these two are simply decorated with animal motifs, one with tiny serpent heads and the other with handles cast in the form of little sea horses.

Domestic silver was as important to Spanish colonials in South America as in Guatemala or Mexico. A custom which demonstrates the esteem in which it is still held was photographed recently for *National Geographic* in front of the colonial church of San Francisco in La Paz, Bolivia. It shows women arranging treasured heirloom silver around the portal in a glittering arch reminiscent of the silver displays with which colonial guilds and *cofradías* (religious fraternities) celebrated the festival of their patron, San Eloy.[38]

Cofradías were special status organizations for men within the church. Not all guild members were admitted to the *cofradía* but it was restricted to silversmiths, many of whom secured lucrative commissions and important positions in the church through its influence. In a Roman Catholic society this meant that they were important members of the community, as indeed they were. In fact, silversmithing in colonial times was called the "noble art" and its organizations were among the most affluent in society, able to present elaborate festivals and bullfights and to provide pensions for aged or disabled members.[39]

We are indebted to the late David Thornburg for most of the Bolivian pieces in the collections. Some are admittedly reproductions, a fact which serves our purpose well because they provide an opportunity to compare copies with colonial pieces. A glance reveals startling differences between two reproductions (Fig. 38-B) and an eighteenth century original (Fig. 36-B). All three represent the typical Bolivian colonial style, which often used different shapes for tops and bottoms of objects and had distinctive conventionalized borders, such as these leaf-and-fold designs. Greater elaboration was added with cast handles, richly and imaginatively composed from floral, leaf, animal and human forms.

The handle on the eighteenth century cup (Fig. 36-B) is a splendid example of this kind of decoration. Here, a tiny human figure lies supine along the top edge above a beautifully modeled pomegranate blossom.

Its deeply tooled leaf-and-fold border, also composed of the pomegranate motif, makes those on the reproductions (Fig. 38-B) look superficial. It is difficult to distinguish details of the fish effigy handles on the copies; their narrow borders are but inept attempts to duplicate the precise beading around the top and bottom of the original. In addition to these purely visual distinctions there is a radical variation in intrinsic elements: weights (proportionately), color, patina and surface textures.

These same distinctions characterize an Andean footed goblet (Fig. 38-A) with inferior cast elements which indicate that it is probably late nineteenth century. Its base and bowl, however, are of high enough quality to have been the work of a skilled colonial craftsman, so it is possible that this is one of those genuine old pieces which were unfortunately remodeled to conform to a more popular style during Republican times. These cast elements, compared to the stem of another footed goblet (Fig. 37), which is stamped with a number like the eighteenth century Argentine stirrups (Fig. 54-A), points up the difference in workmanship between much colonial and postcolonial silver.

Silver tea cups and saucers are rarely found in collections of old silver. They were introduced in the late seventeenth century along with other articles for serving tea and coffee, but lost popularity in the eighteenth century when it became apparent that metal cups were not suitable for hot beverages. Earliest examples were low and, in the Chinese manner, without handles. Soon, however, one- and two-handled silver cups were made in the same shapes as those adopted by porcelain factories.[40]

There is only one plain saucer and few cups in the collections. All cups, with the possible exception of one not illustrated, are nineteenth century. One is a medicine cup (Fig. 34-B) and another (Fig. 39-B) was probably a child's mug. The medicine cup is stamped with a small upright serpent and the letters "ER&N" with a pinhead size head of Hermes, the export stamp of France in the late nineteenth century. Other cups illustrated have bases of various shapes. One (Fig. 39-A) is stamped with the Mexican marks used after 1895 and, since its cast handle is so like those on a two-handled example (Fig. 40-A), it can be assumed that they are of the same place and period. A very good reproduction of a neoclassic urn style (Fig. 40-B*) is stamped with obviously false marks.

One example of a *sahumador* (incense burner) was collected by agents of the I. B. M. Corporation in Chile. This article played a peculiar role in South American colonial society described graphically by Richard Ahlborn:

It was, however, the use of incense that brought ladies of all classes out of their homes and into direct participation in the popular religious processions that continue to this day. The incense burners of Peru held a position in religio-domestic activities comparable to that of the monstrances of Mexico in religio-civil festivals. A variety of architectural, plant and animal forms were worked into lidded containers 6 to 8 inches high. These silver containers were carried from salon to clothes closet to carriage and, on foot, into parades of religious sisterhoods. Returning to the well-to-do home, large incense burners and brazier combinations were found on the dining table and in the grand salon.[41]

Sahumadores, among the most imaginative of Spanish Colonial objects, were made in an almost unlimited variety of forms and techniques. Animals and birds, especially horses, llamas, deer, bulls, lions, turkeys and peacocks, were executed in fine filigree or cast and decorated to every degree of elaboration. Most of them stood on small trays or bases for ease in handling. This one (Fig. 41), a cast and tooled turkey standing on a twig, is an excellent example of the Republican period (c. 1820–1900) when emphasis was placed on native subject matter. Its lid, which was probably attached with a chain in the customary way, is lost.

Largely because of the Field Collection, New Mexico has an unusually fine selection of old silver mugs. The form evolved from the beaker which, in turn, descended from the ancient drinking horn made from a straight section of ox-horn with one end stopped up. Silver beakers had achieved a definitive form, with straight sides that spread at the top, in England and the Low Countries by Elizabethan times. By the late seventeenth century sides were flared and bottoms were molded. In the eighteenth century they were largely replaced by earthenware and china cups, except for those made into mugs and tankards by the addition of handles.[42]

There is only one plain beaker without handles in the collections (Fig. 45-B), but good evidence exists that several of the sixteen mugs in the Field Collection were originally old beakers to which handles were added later. An example of the latter has a double-headed serpent handle (Fig. 42) with the date 1866 inscribed on one side and the monogram "C. G. A." on the other. Both handle and mug are expertly crafted but are put together with crude soldering, indicating that the person who assembled the parts was not the one who made either of them. Prefabricated handles were stock items in many shops, so this one was probably bought, inscribed and attached to a much older beaker.

Indeed, this mug, without the handle, has all the characteristics of a seventeenth century piece, including the old-style bottom which was made separately and attached to stop up one end like a drinking horn. According to

Wyler, by the time of Charles II of England (1660–1685) bottoms were usually molded, as in a pair of matched mugs in the Field Collection (Fig. 45-A).[43]

The very large mug, or tankard, which Mrs. Field bought from Don Salomón Luna (Fig. 43) discussed earlier in relation to the de Vargas will of 1704, has a similar bottom. Rough soldering (visible in the photograph) again indicates that the handle was attached some time after the beaker was made. Since it fits de Vargas' description of his tankard, conforms consistently to early seventeenth century characteristics, and was purchased from a descendant of one of de Vargas' associates, the temptation is great to identify it as his. Without specific identifying marks, however, this cannot be firmly established.

By the end of the seventeenth century, France had become the artistic center of Europe. Styles popularized there were soon adopted by other countries and passed on to their colonies. Such was the case with tulip-shaped tumblers, which replaced straight-sided or flared beakers.[44] One of the three examples in the collections (Fig. 44) is footed and has a simply decorated handle typical of the classical revival.

Another original and distinctive form of Spanish Colonial silver, the *maté* cup, was probably the most widely used specialty article in South America. Tradition has it that Jesuit missionaries introduced the custom of drinking tea made from a variety of holly *(Ilex paraguayensis)* through a sipper called a *bombilla*. They had learned about the herb's unusual properties from the Indians who chewed its green leaves as a stimulant.[45]

The first *bombillas* were made with a small filter of woven vegetable fibers fastened to the immersed end to strain the brew. Later, *bombillas* made from silver were standardized into three parts: a mouthpiece, a tube and a filter. Evidently both *matés* and *bombillas* challenged the imaginations of silversmiths, for they fashioned them with almost unbelievable ingenuity from combinations of silver and other materials as well as from the metal alone. The *bombilla* in the I. B. M. Collection (Fig. 47-B) is one of the simpler styles. More elegant ones were created with tubes in all kinds of fanciful shapes: spirals, corkscrews, curves, countercurves, twisted ropes, turned balusters and loops. Mouthpieces and filter shapes were also varied from silver copies of the early woven ones to serpent heads with colored jewels for eyes.[46]

All five *maté* cups illustrated are from colonial Peru. Two (Fig. 46-A & 48-B) represent the native Andean style of the colonial period. Notable differences between these early pieces and nineteenth century Republican variations are chiefly a matter of emphasis. Local motifs, such as turkey claw feet and birds, dominate as they do in Republican examples. However, the Indian hunter on one colonial *maté* (Fig. 48-B) is observed in an everyday activity, sighting his quarry from the top of the handle, not in the posed "noble" stance of the Inca on the Republican candelabrum (Fig. 17). Both Andean style *matés* are carved gourds in silver mountings, the upper and lower sections fastened together with hinged silver straps. Handles simulate curled "button ends" of gourds, with the hunter replacing the button on the smaller one.

The gourd motif was extremely popular for *maté* cup handles. It is used again on a Bolivian example (Fig. 47-A) which was given to the museum by Mary Cabot Wheelwright. Another from the *altiplano* (Fig. 46-B) has two handles with stylized condors on top. Both are decorated with typical Bolivian scrimshaw borders composed of flower and leaf designs. A more sophisticated *maté* (Fig. 48-A) is composed of a coconut section set on a petal base made out of thick sheet metal. Its two side handles are cast but the one on the lid is, like the base, cut from sheet silver. Many *matés* had lids, some with holes through which *bombillas* were inserted.

It was not until the eighteenth century that the word "cutlery" came to have the meaning it does today, when various articles used for serving meals developed the shapes, sizes and proportions of modern pieces.[47] Knives and spoons are known to have existed since ancient times, but forks are a comparatively recent invention. Some are mentioned in French records as early as the thirteenth century and they were common in Italy by the fifteenth, but other countries did not adopt them until almost two hundred years later. Wyler records an anecdote from an early seventeenth century chronicle which describes the firsthand experiences of a British traveler in Italy in 1620:

> I observed a custom in all those Italian cities and towns through which I passed that is not used in any other country that I saw in my travels, neither do I think that any other nation of Christendom doth use it, but only Italy. The Italian, and also most strangers that are commorant in Italy, do always at their meals use a little fork when they cut their meat . . . their forks being for the most part made of iron or steel, and some of silver, but these are used only by gentlemen. The reason of their curiosity is because the Italian cannot endure by any means to have his dish touched by fingers, seeing that all men's fingers are not alike clean. Hereupon I myself thought to imitate the Italian fashion by this fork cutting of meat, not only while I was in Italy, but also in Germany, and oftentimes in England since I came home.[48]

Forks cannot be dated by number of tines because, though the modern form with four prongs became popular in the eighteenth century, some were still made with only two or three and are still popular for specialty items like cocktail, pickle and meat forks. Of the twenty-three forks in the present collections, only two have three tines. Also, because many eighteenth century flatware designs are still copied, it is sometimes difficult, without hallmarks, to distinguish old from modern pieces. This is, however, only a visual impression for the heft or feel is quite different. Even those which look remarkably contemporary, like the large serving fork and spoon in the Field Collection (Fig. 49), are awkward to use. All Spanish Colonial flatware is notably heavier than modern objects of the same type, and, though it may look the same, is distinguishable by subtle differences in size, shape and balance.

Spanish marks on two tiny salt spoons (Fig. 52-B) were verified for the Museum of New Mexico by the Ortega Antique Shop in Seville as seventeenth century. Five dinner forks and three teaspoons have flat handles like the salt forks, so it is possible that they too are early examples. It is usually easy to identify flatware from Guatemala because it is often decorated with etched floral designs like those on forty-nine forks and spoons collected by Dr. Morley (Fig. 52-A). His two ladles (Fig. 50-A* & B) look like modern pieces.

Four forks in the Museum of New Mexico Collection (Fig. 51-A) have an interesting history. They were dug up a few years ago when workmen were putting in a utility trench in front of the old Governor's Palace in Santa Fe. Failing to see any value in them, the laborers gave them to an observer, Mr. John Wallace, who later donated them to the museum. The one on the right in the illustration is stamped with a "Z" superimposed with an "o" which resembles the strange unidentified mark discussed earlier (compare to Fig. 27-A). The similarity, however, is only superficial because this mark can be read as a "Z" and the other one cannot. The spoon is not hallmarked but it matches six forks in the Field Collection which are stamped with Chief Assayer Cayetano Buitrón's marks (1823–43).

No doubt some, perhaps a great deal, of domestic silver is still owned by descendants of Spanish Colonial families. If so, it is to be hoped that such articles will eventually find their way into museum collections, where their beauty and significance in the colonial history of the United States can be enjoyed and appreciated by the general public.

FOOTNOTES

[1] George Kubler, *Time's Reflection and Colonial Art* (1968 Winterthur Conference Report. Winterthur, Delaware: Henry Francis du Pont Winterthur Museum, 1969), p. 11.

[2] Edward Wenham, *The Practical Book of American Silver* (Philadelphia and New York: J. B. Lippincott Company, 1949), p. 31.

[3] Stéphane Faniel (ed.), *French Art of the 18th Century* (New York: Simon & Shuster, 1957), p. 33.

[4] App. II, Fig. 94, No. 18, this study.

[5] Lawrence Anderson, *The Art of the Silversmiths in Mexico 1519–1936* (New York: Oxford University Press, 1941), pp. 232–33.

[6] Check Anderson's Table of Equivalents for values of *reales* and *marcos*.

[7] Ibid., p. 122.

[8] José Torre Revello, *La orfebrería colonial en Hispanoamerica y particularamente en Buenos Aires* (Buenos Aires: Editorial Huarpes, S. A., 1945), p. 41.

[9] Manuel Romero de Terreros y Vinent, *Las artes industriales en la Nueva España* (México, D. F.: Librería de Pedro Robredo, 1923), pp. 18–19.

[10] Anderson, Vol. I, p. 232.

[11] Ibid., pp. 344–413.

[12] Seymour B. Wyler, *The Book of Old Silver* (New York: Crown Publishers, 1937), pp. 30–33.

[13] C. C. Oman, *English Domestic Silver* (London: A. & C. Black, Ltd.), 1934, pp. 147–167.

[14] Hector Umberto Samayoa Guevara, *Los gremios de artesanos en la Ciudad de Guatemala* (1524-1821) (Guatemala: Editorial Universitaria, 1962), p. 23.

[15] Ibid., pp. 25 & 29.

[16] Samayoa Guevara, "El gremio de plateros de la Ciudad de Guatemala y sus ordenanzas, (1524-1821)," *Antropología e historia de Guatemala*, Vol. IX, No. I (January, 1957), 20.

[17] Alfredo Taullard, *Platería sudamericana* (Buenos Aires: Peuser, Ltda., 1941), Figs. 146, 150 & 155.

[18] Emilio Harth-Terre, *Silver and Silversmiths of Peru*, (Exhibition Catalogue, *Three Centuries of Peruvian Silver*. Washington, D. C. & New York: Smithsonian Institution & Metropolitan Museum of Art, 1968), p. 26.

[19]Modesto Bargalló, *La minaría y la metalurgia en la America Española durante la época colonial* (Mexico-Buenos Aires: Fondo de Cultura Economica, 1955), pp. 74-75.

[20]Taullard, pp. 25-32.

[21]Carlos Neuhaus Ugarteche, *Treasures of Peruvian Antiquity* (Exhibition Catalogue, *Three Centuries of Peruvian Silver*. Washington, D.C. & New York: Smithsonian Institution & Metropolitan Museum of Art, 1968), p. 16.

[22]Check Anderson's Table of Equivalents.

[23]Carlos Pizano y Saucedo, *Platería, siglo XX* (Guadalajara, Mexico: Jalisco en el Arte Series, Planeaceón y Promoción, S. A., 1960), pp. 6-8.

[24]Anderson, Vol. I, pp. 235-236.

[25]Ibid., pp. 395-400.

[26]Taullard, Fig. 299, No. 5.

[27]Richard E. Ahlborn, *Domestic Silver in Colonial Mexico and Comments on Peru* (1968 Winterthur Conference Report. Winterthur, Delaware: Henry Francis du Pont Winterthur Museum, 1969), p. 38.

[28]Anderson, Vol. I, p. 273.

[29]Ibid., p. 277.

[30]Ibid., p. 305.

[31]Check App. II, this study.

[32]John Lloyd Stephens, *Incidents of Travel in Central America, Chiapas and Yucatan*, Vol. II (New York: Harper & Brothers, 1841), p. 225.

[33]D. Artemio de Valle-Arizpe, "Ladrones sacrilegos y plateros inquisitoriados," *Arte y plata* (October, 1945), 15.

[34]1968 Winterthur Conference Report, p. 46.

[35]List of cities with *Cajas Reales* in late 18th. c., App. III, p. 198, this study.

[36]Anderson, Vol. I, p. 360.

[37]John E. Sunder (ed.), Collected by Clyde and Mae Porter, *Matt Field on the Santa Fe Trail* (Norman, Oklahoma: University of Oklahoma Press, 1960), p. 259.

[38]San Eloy was a Christian saint who was also a silversmith. He was born in 587 near Limoges, France. Was appointed court silversmith and director of the Paris mint by King Clotario II and was Bishop of Noyon when he died in 665.

[39]Ibid., p. 31.

[40]Wyler, p. 32.

[41]Ahlborn, p. 41.

[42] Wyler, pp. 47-48.
[43] Ibid.
[44] Faniel, p. 100.
[45] Taullard, p. 61.
[46] Ibid., Figs. 235-272.
[47] Faniel, p. 92.
[48] Wyler, p. 75.

CHAPTER V

ACCESSORIES AND GEAR

Of the sixteen accessory items in the collections, eight are from the northern part of colonial Mexico. These are part of the selection reserved for discussion of provincial styles in Chapter VI. The eight presented in this section are all from South America except two household items from Mexico.

That so few articles of this type were found in these collections does not indicate that such things were not popular in colonial Mexico. Northern provincial ladies loved decorative articles for personal use and bric-a-brac for their homes as much as those elsewhere in the Spanish Colonial world. The distribution is probably due more to preference of collectors than to the absence of such material, because New Mexican men, whom Arthur Woodward graphically describes, were possibly more fond of silver ornaments than were their ladies:

> We know that the Spaniard delighted in an ostentatious display of wealth, which often manifested itself in the personal adornment of his clothing, weapons, and horse trappings. This love of finery was not confined to any one class alone. It has been remarked that the Mexican dandy of the 18th. and early 19th. century might not have a peso in his pocket, but his hat and clothes were profusely decorated with silver and gold, thus creating the impression that the wearer was a man of wealth and substance.[1]

The two pieces from Mexico are religio-domestic. Both a small tray with uptilted ends (Fig. 53-A*) and a silver candle snuffer (Fig. 53-B*), could have been used satisfactorily in a church. The latter is, in fact, like those on Fray Benavides' mission supply list of 1626, discussed in Chapter II. They are presented here because they form part of the Morley collection of table silver. E. Boyd believes, because the snuffers fit the tray so well, that they were bought to be used together. If so, the snuffers can probably be dated by the tray which is stamped with the genuine marks of Chief Assayer Antonio Forcada y La Plaza, who served between 1791 and 1818 (App. II, Fig. 89, No. 11), and an illegible silversmith's mark.

A small memento (Fig. 53-C), probably made in highland Peru in the eighteenth century, also has religious significance. Its central element is made from a nut intricately carved with a complicated design which, like that on its silver mounting, resembles decorative *maté* cups produced in the *altiplano* at that time.[2] Miniscule lettering, carved around the top and bottom of the nut, *"Obsequio me padre José Tapía"* and *"Su ijo [hijo] Benjamin Tapía"* translates, "A gift to my father José Tapía" and "His son Benjamín Tapía."

According to Taullard, two pairs of stirrups (Fig. 54-A & B) are gentlemen's styles from the coastal area of Argentina. One pair, complete with rawhide strap and strap-guides, is typical of some parts of the Province of Buenos Aires. They are fashioned from a single piece of silver and inlaid with gold flowers surrounded by chased leaves around a heart-shaped escutcheon, and probably were designed to hold a name, monogram or personal insignia. Each of the four silver strap-guides, and both stirrups, are stamped with the figure "900" and the name "J. OTERO." The second pair of stirrups, a typical *porteño* (city of Buenos Aires) style, are made from hollowed sections of horn mounted in plain silver rims with threads of beading around the outsides.[3]

Gauchos who worked the great ranches of Argentina are among the most colorful of colonial figures. Only their northern counterparts, American cowboys, have rivaled them as subject matter for romantic literature, legend and music. Articles made to decorate their clothing, gear and weapons form a large body of art unique in the history of silversmithing.

A large belt buckle (Fig. 55) with buttons made from six eight-*reales* pieces is one such object. Presumably the six coins are alike, but the date, 1671, can be deciphered on only three. They are attached to a decorated central medallion by flat metal straps. This style of buckle was very popular on the pampas. They were made with two, three, four or six coins fastened to either side of a central element with flexible links, straps or chains. The coins were slipped through slits in the ends of, or loops attached to, fitted leather belts which were usually wider across the back than in front. Leather sections were often further decorated with silver and tooling, creating a tempting show of wealth which the *gaucho* wore strapped around his waist.[4]

The *gaucho's* favorite weapon, the *bola,* streaks across the pages of South American history from ancient to modern times. *Bolas,* thrown with deadly accuracy by the Indians, were one of the ruder surprises encountered by the first Spaniards who came into present-day Argentina and neighboring countries. First news of this strange weapon reached Europe from the Spanish chronicler Gonzalo Fernández de Oviedo, who died in 1557. Others mentioned it later, among them Don Diego Rodríquez de Valdés, governor for the viceroyalty of the territories of the Río de la Plata, who wrote in a letter to the king dated May 20, 1599:

> They are not people whom one can trust: they fight with bow and arrows and with two balls of stone tied by a cord about two arm-spans long, and holding a ball in one hand, they throw them with such skill that at one hundred paces they entangle a man and a horse, and in the air, some large birds like ducks and other similar ones . . .[5]

Spanish settlers soon adopted the *bola* and a particular kind of *gaucho* came into being. He was the *boleador,* an expert in the art of using the *bola.* The Indians had always carried *bolas* on their backs, but a *boleador* rode with his hanging from his saddle or tied to his belt for much the same purpose and in the same way the North American cowboy carried his lariat. The *bola* was more than a weapon; it also was the *gaucho's* most valuable working tool. Not only could he kill a lion or a man with an accurate throw to the head, he could also entangle the legs of running steers and other animals, bringing them to the ground without injury.

Primitive *bolas* were made with either one or two stone balls attached to long strands of leather or animal intestines. There were disadvantages to both forms, particularly the two-ball variety, which had to be grasped in the center of the "nerve" (cord) between the two balls, thus halving its projectional span. The problem was solved by fastening a shorter cord at the middle of the original nerve. To this a third *bola,* which fit into the palm of the hand, was attached. Because this type seemed to shoot like stars as the *boleador* whirled it over his head and threw it, it came to be known as *Las Tres Marías* (the three Marías) after the three stars in the belt of Orion.[6]

The Museum of New Mexico example, a set of three bolas (Fig. 56-A), was no doubt the pride of an Argentine *gaucho* in the eighteenth century.

Though its ivory balls with silver mounts and swivels are quite sophisticated, they were no less efficient than common ones made by pouring
melted lead around U-shaped pieces of metal placed upside down in various sized eggshells so the closed ends projected from the top of the ball
to form eyelets through which cords could be passed. In this example
the third cord is lashed to the middle of a twisted rawhide nerve, creating
a solid hand grip for throwing *Las Tres Marías*.[7]

FOOTNOTES

[1]Arthur Woodward, *A Brief History of Navajo Silversmithing*
(Flagstaff, Arizona: Northern Arizona Society of Science and Art, 1946),
p. 9.

[2]Alfred Taullard, *Platería sudamericana* (Buenos Aires: Peuser, Ltda.,
1941), compare to Fig. 235, Nos. 5 & 6 and Fig. 238.

[3]Ibid., Fig. 299, Nos. 5 & 6.

[4]Ibid., Figs. 332-337.

[5]Alberto Blasi Brambilla, "The Three Marías," *Américas,* Vol. 21,
No. 7 (July, 1969), 35–36.

[6]Ibid., pp. 35-39.

[7]Ibid.

CHAPTER VI

PROVINCIAL STYLES

All Spanish Colonial art is provincial in that it was produced in areas distant from continental prototypes. When art styles undergo such transmissions, they are modified according to the extent of contact between metropolis and province and the kinds of influences encountered by the parent style in a new locale. This pattern is then repeated between provincial cities and rural areas, especially in regions so extensive and diverse as the several Spanish colonies in the New World. It is this second, localized, transformation of styles, twice removed from points of origin, with which this study is primarily concerned.

Attention is focused on silver from that part of colonial Mexico which in 1777 was established by the Council of the Indies under a special government called the "Commandancy-General of the Interior Provinces."[1] This political division, created to protect New Spain's northern frontiers from hostile Indians, was composed of Sonora, New Mexico and Texas. At that time the last two provinces extended south into modern Mexico to a point about halfway between El Paso and the city of Chihuahua.[2]

According to A. Curtis Wilgus' *Historical Atlas of Latin America,* the loosely defined northern border of this region followed a line north and west from New Orleans to the juncture of the southern borders of Nebraska and Wyoming, then west to the Pacific at San Francisco.[3]

Since there are still no large Mexican centers of population within these boundaries, except border towns whose growth is of recent date, any stylistic developments here must have occurred chiefly within what is now the southwestern part of the United States. Silver plate from this part of colonial Mexico is, for reasons explained in the following discussion, classified in this study as "Northern Provincial."

As George Kubler pointed out in his paper "Time's Reflection and Colonial Art," there are certain characteristics common to all objects made in the colonial worlds of America. One has to do with the fact that points at the periphery of colonial systems communicated more with the central metropolis than with each other.[4] For example, Mexico City was influenced by Madrid rather than Guatemala City, Quito, Lima or Buenos Aires, and the same was true of each of these.

Therefore, the common denominator of a provincial style is resemblance to original parent forms. Variations which accumulate as a style moves outward from the center occur within the original stylistic configuration, but crystallize into distinctive regional expressions as the style is transmitted. It is precisely these variations which distinguish one Spanish Colonial style from another.

The following outline of consistent changes in Spanish silver plate as the craft moved from Spain to Mexico City to the northern periphery (New Mexico) will help to clarify those variations upon which the discussion of the Northern Provincial style is based.

TRANSMISSIONS OF SPANISH COLONIAL STYLE

I. SPANISH STYLE

II. PROVINCIAL STYLE AT CENTER (Mexico City).
   Repetition of Spanish forms modified by:
   1. *Greater availability of raw material.* Results:
      a. Heavier than original.
      b. Richer surfaces than original.
   2. *New work force.* Original group transplanted from Spain. Trained succeeding generations. Results: Little self-generated change.
   3. *Local traditions.* Little influence from Indian art forms. Indian craftsmen worked under Spanish or Creole silversmiths.
   4. *Different system of hallmarking.* Results:
      a. Different marks.
      b. Little control (few marks) in early period (1520–1638).
      c. Tax controls enforced with increasing amount of marking (1638–1895).
   5. *New Market.* Spanish social system transplanted to new capital.

Predominantly urban. Results: Little change due to taste or requirements of buyers. Continued reliance of Creoles on European forms.

III. PROVINCIAL STYLE AT PERIPHERY.
Repetition of Spanish forms modified by:
1. *New work force.* Often unskilled with fewer and sometimes inferior tools. Results:
   a. Increasing exposure of method of manufacture. Visibility of tool marks.
   b. Increasing inaccuracies. Asymmetry and lack of finish.
2. *Decreasing familiarity with original forms.* Results:
   a. Overcompensation. Objects heavier and more strongly articulated than necessary.
   b. Simplification of forms.
3. *Local traditions.* Some influence. Results:
   Some modification of form and decoration.
4. *Hallmarking.* Less as distance from center increases. Results: No marks in interior provinces (extreme periphery).
5. *New market.* Less sophisticated society. Predominantly rural. Results:
   a. Fewer specialized articles.
   b. Emphasis on functionalism.

The sum total of these variations resulted in the creation of articles in the Interior Provinces with quite different characteristics from those of central or southern Mexico. This fact, added to the accidents of history which transferred the larger part of this region to the United States, seems to require that the style of these objects be differentiated by name from that of its southern counterparts.

Three of the twenty-three Northern Provincial objects in the collections are not illustrated because of similarity. Of the twenty photographed, five are ecclesiastic, thirteen are domestic and two are accessories. One *tabaquera* which was probably made in the United States (Fig. 79-A) is included because it was undoubtedly decorated in New Mexico.

In order to facilitate comparisons, illustrations of Northern Provincial objects are mounted on the same page with, or very near to, examples known to have come from rural sections in other parts of Spanish America. For example: a crown for a small seated *Santo Niño,* which was given to the Museum of New Mexico by Father Burke of San Juan Pueblo, New Mexico (Fig. 56-B), contrasts strikingly with one for a large Virgin (Fig. 57-A) collected by an agent of the museum in rural Colombia.

Both are naive interpretations of a traditional ecclesiastic form and both were unskillfully cut from pieces of flat sheet metal—but here the resemblance ends. The *Niño's* crown clearly demonstrates that simplification so consistently a characteristic of articles made on the extreme northern periphery. The Colombian piece, however, because that area was more closely related to colonial centers, is an earnest attempt to recreate a florid urban style. It is composed of a decorated circlet with twenty-seven triangular cut-outs, all of which were originally topped with scored circles, crossed strips of sheet metal on which winged cherubs are perched, and a cross. Most of its small castings have been lost and replaced with poor pot metal reproductions. Nothing as ambitiously ornate as this was found in New Mexico.

Eloquent simplicity also characterizes an oblong tray (Fig. 57-B) which, according to Mary Lester Field's note came ''. . . from the Church in Old Town, from the priest in charge.'' The ''Old Town'' to which she referred is that part of Albuquerque which stands today, a living memorial to history, clustered around its plaza on the site where it was established in 1706 by Interim Governor Francisco Cuervo y Valdes and named for the Viceroy of New Spain, the Duke of Alburquerque. The church, San Felipe de Neri, was built in 1793 to replace the original mission built when the town was founded. Although the tray is smoothly planished, it is crudely soldered to its base, indicating that it was probably made locally.

In frontier areas domestic silver was often adapted to serve several purposes. Such is the case with two six-lobed plates (Fig. 62-A & B) which obviously derive from the internationally popular style of an example from Mexico City (Fig. 31-A). The urban example is 1.9 cm. (three-fourths of an inch) deep. The two provincial ones, one *Norteño* and the other Northern Provincial, are almost one and three-quarter inches—sufficiently deep to serve as soup or vegetable bowls as satisfactorily as for plates.

Although definitely contrary to Catholic practice, this same utilitarian approach seems to have extended to ecclesiastic silver in New Mexico. Fray Dominguez' description in 1776 of the uses to which parts of the chalice in the Mission Church of St. Thomas in Abiquiú were put ''. . . but the chalice is in three pieces, and one of them, for it is a loan by the settlers, is used for a little shrine they have'' not only proves such usage but also that silver articles were provided for the church by local people.[5]

The chalice described by Father Dominguez was probably very like one used by the Franciscans in New Mexico before 1820 (Fig. 58). It too is in three parts, two of which could have been used "for a little shrine" like the one at Abiquiú. Its base is fastened to the bottom section of the stem so it could have been detached and used as a low candlestick. The cup, with or without the central stem, would have made a nice vase for flowers in front of a holy image. In order to satisfy the church's requirement that those parts of sacristy vessels which touched the Elements be made of gold, the inside of the cup is gold washed. These were usually gold plated in chalices for wealthier churches.

A neoclassic incense boat (Fig. 59-A) is rather badly damaged. Crudities of manufacture, such as rough soldering where the handles are attached, suggest a local silversmith. It is probably late nineteenth century because it would have taken at least twenty-five years for a style popular in Mexico City early in the century to have reached New Mexico. The lids are double hinged from the top instead of from either side of a spoon trough, as in the Museum of New Mexico example (Fig. 13-A). A little hole, visible in the photograph, is probably a scar where a chain and spoon were attached. The initials "R. N.," hand-inscribed on the rim, are very like those on one of the Field mugs (Fig. 75), so it can be assumed that both objects at one time belonged to the same person.

Two small objects, the Sandoval pyx (Fig. 60) compared to the Indian peace medal in Chapter II and a *Norteño* locket made from a nut encased in silver (Fig. 59-B), have narrow borders scratched with a burin, like *buriladas*. This kind of decoration is a perfect example of provincialism, typifying the kind of transformation which occurs when an unskilled artisan attempts to duplicate the impression created by fine beaded borders (compare to Fig. 22-B). The pyx has two lids hinged on opposite sides, one etched with Christ's monogram and the other with "MAR" (Maria), topped by a fanciful crown. Its fabricated parts are so superior to the decorations that it seems likely it was made elsewhere and decorated locally. Although the locket, like much Spanish Colonial jewelry, had some religious significance, a monogramed heart opposite the cross suggests a sentimental ornament rather than a piece of ecclesiastic jewelry.

A pair of small bull *sahumadores* (Fig. 61-A) typify the simplicity of *Norteño* objects compared to other South American silver (compare to Fig. 41). Unlike their sophisticated urban counterparts, which often depicted animals in action, these provincial examples express a stolid immobility, emphasized by smoothly modeled planes and little articulation at the joints. They are simply decorated with outlined saddles and flowers on the shoulders. Although skillfully cast, mold marks are visible—especially along a line between the mouth and ears. Their tails, which may have been looped carrying chains, are missing.

As pointed out earlier, articles from northwest Argentina compare well with New Mexican pieces because both styles developed under similar circumstances. They represent isolated, predominantly rural societies, far removed from metropolitan influences. Artisans in such regions were likely to have been blacksmiths like the one mentioned in Chapter II who taught the first Navajo to work silver. These often worked with the clumsy tools used for iron and were generally unfamiliar with refined prototypes of articles they attempted to copy.

Despite this common background there were significant differences which led to recognizable distinctions between *Norteño* and Northern Provincial objects. One of the most important resulted from differing compositions of the two work forces. From earliest times Spaniards in South America utilized the special talents of Indian metalworkers, who often possessed more knowledge and skill than European craftsmen. They were admitted to silversmith's guilds and worked as peers, first with Spanish and later with Creole artisans. As early as 1572 special provisions were made in the Ordinances of Government for the City of Cuzco for Indian *plateros* to have their own houses in Santiago Apostol, a township across the river from the city where they worked.[6]

According to Taullard, Indian *plateros* from upper Peru came in the seventeenth century to the towns of Jujuy and Salta, just below the border of modern Bolivia, where they worked for the Marqués de Valle and other wealthy families. One of the most important eighteenth century silversmiths in Salta, Fabián Espada, was the son of a Spaniard and a *chola* (half-breed). This is not to imply that all South American silversmiths were Indians, but simply that they were an important part of the colonial work force.[7]

This was not true in New Mexico. Some observers have assumed that New Mexican Colonial silver was made by the Indians, as did Elisabeth Moses, who wrote the catalogue description of a few of Mrs. Field's pieces when they were exhibited by the M. H. de Young Memorial Museum in San Francisco, California, in October, 1938:

The Spanish American silver from the handsome collection of Mrs. Neill B. Field of Albuquerque, New Mexico, offers a most excellent example of a rare phase of American silver-making. . . . Whether the consistent plainness should be attributed to the immaturity of the craftsmen—some of the pieces were undoubtedly made by Indians trained by the Spanish colonists—or whether the objects were created in a plain and strong manner because they had to be transported from one location to another, we do not know.[8]

Actually, the simplicity and strength of these objects resulted from stylistic influences outlined earlier, not because they were made by Indians or had to be transported from place to place. There is no evidence of any kind to indicate that Indians in New Mexico learned the art of silversmithing before the 1850s, some thirty years after the close of the colonial period.[9] Since the Navajo, Zuñi and other Pueblo people in the state are now internationally recognized as expert silversmiths, it is probable that, had they worked earlier, many Northern Provincial objects would have been more skillfully executed.

Twelve pieces from Argentina *(Norteño),* three from rural Mexico (present boundaries), one from rural Bolivia, four from Colombia and one from San Blas Islands are illustrated. These twenty-one provincial objects from other parts of the Spanish Colonial world form our basis of comparison with the twenty Northern Provincial examples photographed. If our selection from other areas is representative, there can be no doubt concerning distinctions between their local styles and that of New Mexico. Differences in expertise and impact of native forms account for many distinctive characteristics. This can be clearly demonstrated by comparing several articles illustrated in this section.

Two bowls, one Northern Provincial and one *Norteño* (Fig. 66-A & B), derive from popular European fluted or lobed styles. Each, for different reasons, is far removed from its original form. The New Mexican piece (Fig. 66-A) deviates because the bottom was made separately and attached. This flattened the flutes and permitted only a semblance of flare at the top, which is further minimized by the addition of small handles on which ball finials are placed in different positions. This method was probably used, quite simply, because the artisan lacked the skill to "raise" flutes gracefully from the bottom, as in urban Mexican prototypes (Figs. 32-A & 35-B). Naturally, the result is a radically different looking object, even more so than another attempt at fluting as seen in the largest bowl in the Field Collection (Fig. 65-A). Here the original form is more closely observed, but shallow scoring from bottom to top actually created supporting ribs, not flutes. Even this was not accomplished without the additional support of a base, an element not present on either of the bowls from Mexico City. Both provincial bowls obviously owe their different visual impacts to lack of skill, not to influence from Indian or other local traditions.

Just the opposite is true of the *Norteño* bowl (Fig. 66-B). Here the original lobed shape (Fig. 35-B) is quite literally transformed into an Indian pottery "squash" form by broadening the lobes and extending them to a small base completely hidden under the bowl. This transformation can best be appreciated by studying side and top views (Fig. 5). Although visible tool marks reveal the hand of a comparatively unskilled silversmith, its almost perfect symmetry indicates complete familiarity with the form, a fact obviously not true of the artisan who tried to retain a Spanish style in another *Norteño* bowl (compare Figs. 68-A and 31-B).

Indian pottery forms undoubtedly served as models for provincial silversmiths in both areas, regardless of ethnic backgrounds of the artisans. The influence of pottery, however, is more direct and pronounced in *Norteño* objects like the squash bowl than in those from the northern provinces. For example, a South American jar (Fig. 67-A) is an almost perfectly reproduced globular Indian olla (water jar) while a Northern Provincial bowl (Fig. 67-B) is a Europeanized adaptation of an Indian pottery shape. The olla is foreign to Spanish silver, but two-handled bowls are common. Only the contour of the Northern Provincial example distinguishes it from an urban style (compare to Fig. 33-A).

These two objects also demonstrate obvious differences in surface textures which result from varying degrees of skill. Taullard reproduces four *Norteño* ollas of different types, two of which have wedding ring handles like this one, and two others just as expertly crafted.[10] These may have been made in Salta or Jujuy where, as noted earlier, trained silversmiths from Peru had settled. The fact that there were no such skilled professional groups within the province of New Mexico except, perhaps, for a few in Santa Fe in the nineteenth century, accounts for many distinctions—including the rough surface of the Field bowl compared to the *Norteño* olla—between the two styles.

A *Norteño* gravy or sauce boat (Fig. 65-B) testifies to a second condition which affected, in a different way, the styles of the two regions. Raw materials were much more readily available in northwest Argentina than in what is now the southwestern part of the United States where, because of the distance from Mexican mines, articles made of silver were status symbols owned by a relatively small privileged class. Silver was, in contrast, so plentiful in the *Norteño* region that it could be used generously for a great many everyday objects. Enrique Abeledo emphasized this point in a recently published article on Argentine folk arts:

> In spite of its name (meaning ''shining like silver''), Argentina was not rich in precious metals. But gold and silver were abundant in Upper Peru (today Bolivia), a zone that formed part of the Viceroyalty of the River Plate and that supplied the precious metal over a period of centuries. Colonial dinner services, the only evidence of wealth in the home, were made with silver from Potosí. Foreign travelers were

SQUASH SHAPED BOWL (two views) — Drawings by Jim Wood.

Figure 5

amazed on contemplating the utensils worked in silver that the colonists in these humble villages possessed. Platters, kettles, plates, jars, matés, incense burners, candelabra, candle holders, table settings, mirror frames, chamber pots, inkwells, and so on have been passed on until we can see them today in public museums or private collections.[11]

It is evident from the above description that there were more specialized articles in the *Norteño* repertoire of forms than in Northern Provincial. This handsome sauce boat, which would be a faithful reproduction of an urban style if the spout were not higher than the body of the bowl, is not only a good example of such specialization but also represents a typically *Norteño* extravagent use of silver. It weighs well over 963.9 gr. (2 pounds, 2 ounces), a fantastic weight for so small a piece.

The same characteristic is evident in a 2.35 kg. (5 pound 3 ounce) *Norteño* tray (Fig. 61-B) of the type called a *charola,* meaning that it is the right size and shape to hold several serving dishes at one time. Insofar as style is concerned, it is closer to a deep platter in the Field Collection (Fig. 63-A) than were the bowls and jars just compared. Mrs. Field called her platter a ''tureen''—a reasonable description when one notes its proportions: large enough and shallow enough for a meat platter yet deep enough to hold gravies, vegetables, or even soups. In fact, a sharply tooled edge around the top of the bowl section seems to have been executed with the deliberately utilitarian intention of making it safe for serving liquids. The result is a modification of style to one controlled by sharp angles instead of smoothly modulated transitions from plane to plane, as in the original form (compare to Fig. 27-A).

The platter, like the *Norteño* tray (Fig. 61-B), exhibits asymmetrical variations of form and the wonderfully sensual surfaces produced by hammer marks and inaccuracies of tooling. These supposed defects heighten, rather than diminish, the viewer's feeling for the organic strength of pure, precious metal. These same qualities characterize two dual-purpose serving dishes from rural Colombia (Figs. 63-B & 64-A). Both are shallow lobed variations of the same popular eighteenth century urban style (compare to Fig. 30-A). Neither, however, conforms to traditional shapes. One is a flattened oval and the other is egg-shaped.

A combination pitcher and sauce dish (Fig. 64-B) is so far removed from any particular form that it must be considered a *Norteño* ''original,'' either the product of some artisan's imagination or his inability to handle material consistently. Its bottom half, which is quite monumental and conservative, flares at the top into overlarge, airy scallops much more in keeping with its curvilinear handle than with the bowl to which it is attached. Nevertheless, it approaches genius when considered as a functional design. Any of its four broad flares makes a perfect cradle to hold ladles or spoons for gravy, sauces, preserves or jellies and is, at the same time, an excellent pouring spout for liquids.

A Northern Provincial bowl (Fig. 68-B) which was probably the cup of a *braserillo*, is obviously overcompensated. A bolt, which must have attached it to a stem or baluster rising from a *braserillo* tray, passes through the bottom and is held by a wingnut. It is hard to imagine, since it won't hold liquids, how else it could have functioned. If this is correct, it was made much larger and deeper than necessary for its purpose (compare to Figs. 32-B & 36-A).

Two late nineteenth century cups are illustrated because they typify the degeneration of provincial silversmithing which occurred in much of Latin America after the colonial period. One from rural Colombia (Fig. 69-A) weighs only 77.96 gr. (2¾ ounces). It is extremely light compared to a colonial cup from New Mexico (Fig. 69-B) with a handle mended by shortening it into an acute angle, which weighs 240.98 gr. (8½ ounces). The Colombian example is a crude copy of a popular European demitasse form. The band of indentations with which it is decorated, however, seems to have been made with a leather-working tool. Two tiny blobs of metal (enlarged in illustration) are so deliberately placed as to suggest that they were intended to deceive an unwary buyer into thinking they were hall-marks—a not uncommon practice after Spanish Colonial silver became valuable as antiques.

A cup from the Lake Titicaca area of Bolivia (Fig. 70) is interesting both historically and stylistically. It was made either during or following the regime of Mariano Melgarejo, dictator of Bolivia from 1820 to 1871. A coin bearing his name is sunk into the bottom of the cup, which is fastened to a stem in the manner of its Andean prototype (compared to Fig. 38-A). It may have belonged to a rural priest because, according to Taullard, *copóns* of this shape were used for communion "in small amounts" at bedsides of dying persons.[12] It typifies the Bolivian tradition of making handles in the shapes of animals, birds, or fish. Here, however, it is a simply tooled cut-out, rather than a casting, crudely attached upside down. Regularly spaced milling, much more skillfully executed than other decorations, suggests that another coin was used as a supporting disc between the stem and cup.

Of the six provincial mugs illustrated, four are Northern Provincial and two are *Norteño.* All are simple compared to the urban models from which they derive, but those from New Mexico are plainer than the two from South America. This emphasizes another stylistic distinction revealed by our selection of provincial styles. The Sandoval pyx (Fig. 60) is the only Northern Provincial object which is complicated in any way—and even here it is only a matter of decoration. In contrast, some *Norteño* pieces such as the fluted bowl (Fig. 68-A) and the combination pitcher and sauce dish (Fig. 64-B) are quite complex, as are the Melgarejo cup from rural Bolivia (Fig. 70) and the demitasse cup from Colombia (Fig. 69-A).

Only one Northern Provincial mug has a molded bottom (Fig. 75). The rest were made by wrapping a piece of sheet silver into a cylinder and soldering it to a base which, in each case, is stronger and heavier than necessary. Decorations on all four are restricted to simply designed handmade handles.

No object could speak more eloquently of provincialism than a small straight-sided mug (Fig. 71) in the Field Collection. Its absolute simplicity expresses the integrity of a craftsman who attempted nothing beyond his ability and designed according to his own background and taste. Its small, carefully polished handle suggests, but does not imitate, an Indian feather design. It is attached higher on the mug than would have been done by a more knowledgeable designer, probably only because it pleased the maker to hook one of the feather elements over the top rim. The visual imbalance thus created is not disturbing because actual weight balance is maintained by a base heavy enough to eliminate any danger of tipping.

This forthright approach, difficult to describe in words, characterizes most Northern Provincial silver. Utilitarianism seems to have been the chief consideration, whether an article was to know hard service by a family or to be placed on the head of a holy image, like the tiny crown for the *Santo Niño* from the chapel near San Juan Pueblo (Fig. 56-B). It is exactly what it claims to be—no more and no less. A tremendous respect for material very nearly results in total dependence upon the quality of the precious metal itself. This attitude is poignantly emphasized by the fact that the value of the little crown could not be impaired, even by tying it to the *Niño's* head with a piece of common string (visible in the photograph).

Another Northern Provincial mug (Fig. 73) seems to state, "I am a mug—with a handle big enough for anyone." It is just that, a drinking vessel for a frontier family, without pretense of artistic merit but perfectly conceived and executed to serve its purpose. Mrs. Field, in her hand-written note, stated that it came from the Pinos, a family which has lived in New Mexico since 1747.[13] Don Pedro Bautisto y Pino, one of its most illustrious members, was the province's only delegate to the parliament of Spain in 1813. When he returned he brought back an English carriage in which, anecdotes relate, he proudly traveled the dusty roads of New Mexico—much to the amazement of its provincial populace. The name ''Pino'' is crudely scratched on the bottom of the mug. It probably took the same rough treatment as a broken cup in the Museum of New Mexico Collection (not illustrated) which, according to museum records, belonged to the Delgado family of Santa Fe: ''Family said it had been used for many years as a communal drinking cup, kept outside of kitchen on a bench with water bucket. As each person drank water he banged the cup against the bench by way of 'rinsing' it until it was broken. . . .''[14]

Another of the Field mugs (Fig. 74) is even more obviously utilitarian. Its handle is attached at the top with a bolt and nut on the inside, while a strong connecting element secures it at the bottom. No evidence indicates that its heavy, crudely cut handle was added later, so it was probably made this way originally—a method which suggests that its creator may have been a blacksmith more skilled in working iron than silver. One would think that an object so roughly constructed would have no aesthetic value; this is not true. Such a direct and forceful handling of almost pure silver created an incomparably rich surface which strikes the eye with startling intensity.

Both of the *Norteño* mugs are decorated. They represent two of several styles, including tulip and barrel shapes, which were popular in South America. The one with a massive base and fishtail handle (Fig. 72) is almost exactly the same shape as a *Norteño* mug illustrated by Frederico Oberti in an article in *Arte popular y artesanías tradicionales de la Argentina*.[15] It moves upward gracefully from the base to a rolled edge which forms a strong supporting lip around the top. A row of small punched circles which traces the edges of its handles and base is also used to border the silver mountings of a straight-sided horn mug, the other *Norteño* example (Fig. 76). Here a simply striated horn section is transparently thin, perfectly in keeping with the rows of delicately chiseled scallops which encircle it at top and bottom.

A rather awkward stemmed goblet (Fig. 77) is the only one of its kind in the collections. Its base, stem and cup were made separately and inexpertly put together, exposing the method of manufacture even more obviously than in most Northern Provincial pieces. The cup section is a piece of sheet metal, wrapped around, hammered into shape and soldered with a visible seam. E. Boyd thinks that it was probably used to hold spoons in the middle of the dining table—a custom in New Mexican frontier homes. If so, it is one of the few specialized articles in our selection of Northern Provincial silver.

One other specialized item, a water or wine carafe (Fig. 78), has the rich, velvety patina so characteristic of old silver. A series of dents is so evenly spaced around the bowl as to suggest that it may have been made deliberately for decorative purposes, but otherwise the carafe is perfectly plain.

Decorations, when applied to Northern Provincial objects, were usually restricted to clearly defined patterns, even on personal articles like a *tabaquera* in the Field Collection (Fig. 79-C). Here a central floral motif is enclosed within stamped borders in the style of leather tooling. Another *tabaquera* (Fig. 79-A) probably originated in the eastern part of the United States. It is made of so-called "German silver," a white alloy of zinc, nickel and copper used to make trade articles for the Indians after 1830.[16] It was much prized for its glowing beauty and nontarnishable qualities. Little boxes such as this were often included in the trader's store of trinkets. This one was probably transformed into a *tabaquera* for one "JOSEFA VALDES" in New Mexico because it happened to be the right size and shape to carry her stock of locally grown tobacco, called *ponchi*. Her name is stamped on the lid with individual letters of the type gunsmiths used in pioneer times to mark articles for their customers. It is decorated with a simple geometric flower delineated by stamped concentric circles.

A set of harness buckles, collected in Mexico (Fig. 80-B), probably originated in one of the present-day northern states. This judgment is made on the basis of style. The buckles conform in every way to the stylistic characteristics of Northern Provincial silver: simplicity, tooled decoration, restriction of design area, crude manufacture and exposure of method (note edges of section cut out for buckle element). Another gear ornament, a *concha* (Fig. 80-C), is a borderline example of provincialism. Fairly accurate tooling around the bottom of its central dome indicates that it was made by a capable, but not expert, silversmith, so it probably originated in one of colonial Mexico's northern cities, such as Zacatecas. Its decoration, however, removes it from a Northern Provincial classification. No article from New Mexico is ornamented with embossing or repoussé, as in the flower motifs on this piece.

The harness buckles are actually *conchas* with the centers cut out. *Conchas*, so called because of the resemblance to shells, are ancient decorations for horse trappings which were introduced into Spain by the Moslems as early as the eighth century. They were brought to the New World by the Spaniards and soon became popular decorative ornaments on clothing, hat bands, belts, chaps, boots, and jewelry. Many were plain discs, some were simply decorated, others were cut and tooled into fanciful shapes and designs.[17] *Conchas* are still being made. Indian silversmiths in New Mexico incorporate them into their distinctive jewelry styles.

The last provincial object discussed has no counterpart in Northern Provincial silver. It is a pectoral (Fig. 80-A) of the type worn by Indians in some areas of Mexico, Central and South America. North American Indians wore pectorals, but since they did not learn the art until after the close of the colonial period, theirs were not made of silver. This example is from the San Blas Islands off the north coast of Panama. It consists of a shaped silver plate with an eyelet for a neck cord at the top and a series of dangling coins threaded on a leather thong across the bottom. Raised half-circle motifs which decorate the main section, were produced the same way as the star design on the German silver *tabaquera*—by stamping the background with a tool. On the pectoral the raised pattern is outlined for greater emphasis. Of the twenty-seven coins still attached all are Mexican two-*reales* pieces dated between 1772 and 1807 except one from San Blas, dated 1808. The coins show little evidence of wear, indicating that they were probably assembled on the pectoral early in the nineteenth century.

CONCLUSION:

This analysis of provincial styles has had two objectives: first, to distinguish differences between urban and rural styles in general and second, to differentiate between New Mexico's Northern Provincial style and that of silver from other rural areas of colonial Spanish America.

Because of circumstances under which the five collections were assembled, almost all objects with which New Mexican equivalents were compared came from the Andean area. It seems reasonable to assume that other schools of provincial silver existed and that their analysis might, to some degree, modify conclusions arrived at in this study. Also, as was suggested earlier, further examination of material within the United States might alter the picture somewhat. Subject to these two qualifications, however, the evidence presented here clearly indicates that a Northern Provincial style of colonial silver does indeed exist. Its identification designates silver from the northernmost provinces of New Spain, most of which now lie within the continental boundaries of the United States.

A recapitulation of characteristics of provincial styles, as delineated in this chapter, may prove helpful at this point:

NORTHERN PROVINCIAL:

1. Simplified forms, Spanish in origin.
2. Simple, unsophisticated designs.

ANDEAN (including *Norteño*):

1. Simplified forms, sometimes Indian in origin.
2. Unsophisticated but sometimes pretentious designs.

3. Little decoration.
4. Usually crude. Tool marks visible. Textured surfaces dominant.
5. Much emphasis upon functionalism.
6. Usually overcompensated. Objects heavier and more strongly articulated than necessary.
7. Few specialized articles.
8. No hallmarks.

3. Considerable decoration.
4. Sometimes skilled. Both smooth and textured surfaces.
5. Some emphasis upon functionalism.
6. Often overcompensated. Objects sometimes excessively heavy.
7. Many specialized articles.
8. No hallmarks.

Many of these Northern Provincial characteristics are probably also present, to some degree, in objects made in or near cities of northern Mexico like Chihuahua, Parral, Torreón, Saltillo, Monterrey, or even as far south as Durango and Zacatecas. Classification of objects from these areas as Spanish Colonial or Northern Provincial would depend upon whether they conform more to the style of the center or the periphery. All articles, however, which have been firmly related to the province of New Mexico conform consistently to the stylistic configuration outlined above.

This consistent and distinctive character of New Mexican pieces proves that their classification is not a matter of geography alone. It is also a matter of style. Physical evidence conclusively indicates that they represent that point in the transmission of a parent style when it is modified enough to be transformed into a new and different style which should be recognized as such. Certainly, the assumption of its existence permitted analysis of these five collections with greater clarity than would otherwise have been possible.

Now identified, Northern Provincial silver should take its proper and deserved place as one of the rare and beautiful styles of American colonial art.

FOOTNOTES

[1] Cleve Hallenbeck, *Land of the Conquistadores* (Caldwell, Idaho: The Caxton Printers, Ltd., 1950), p. 238.

[2] Ibid., map, p. 270.

[3]Curtis A. Wilgus, *Historical Atlas of Latin America* (New York: Cooper Square Publishers, Inc., 1967).

[4]George Kubler, *Time's Reflection and Colonial Art* (1968 Winterthur Conference Report. Winterthur, Delaware: Henry Francis du Pont Winterthur Museum, 1969), pp. 7–11.

[5]Chap. III, footnote 2, p. 37, this study.

[6]Emilio Harth-Terre, *Silver and Silversmiths of Peru,* (Exhibition Catalogue, *Three Centuries of Peruvian Silver*. Washington, D. C. & New York: Smithsonian Institution & Metropolitan Museum of Art, 1968), pp. 25–26.

[7]Alfredo Taullard, *Platería sudamericana* (Buenos Aires: Peuser, Ltda., 1941), pp. 57–58.

[8]Elisabeth Moses, *Three Centuries of European and Domestic Silver* (Exhibition Catalogue. San Francisco: M. H. de Young Memorial Museum, October, 1938).

[9]Documentary evidence supporting this data presented in Chap. II, p. 23–24, this study.

[10]Taullard, Figs. 112–113.

[11]Enrique A. Abeledo, "Argentine Folk Arts," *Americas,* Vol. 21, No. 5 (May, 1969), 39.

[12]Taullard, p. 42, illustrated, Fig. 93.

[13]Fray Angelico Chavez, *Origins of New Mexico Families* (Santa Fe, New Mexico: The Historical Society of New Mexico, 1954), p. 258.

[14]Museum of New Mexico, Ledger, Accession No. A. 60. 25-¼.

[15]Frederico Oberti, "Platería," *Arte popular y artesanías tradicionales de la Argentina,* E 6 serie del siglo y medio, (1964), 27, Fig. 3.

[16]Arthur Woodward, *A Brief History of Navajo Silversmithing* (Flagstaff, Arizona: Northern Arizona Society of Science and Art, 1946), p. 7.

[17]Ibid., pp. 21–24.

CANDLESTICKS, Mexico, dated 1729. Museum of New Mexico Collection. Inscription on bases: "SON DE LA ARCHCOERA. DADE S. SMO/DE LA YGLESIA DE ESTA NUEBA BERA CRUZ/AÑO DE 1729." Heights: 55 cm; widths (base): 17 cm; weights: 3.78 kg. and 3.91 kg. Marks:

Figure 6

CANDLESTICKS, Paraguay, c. 1700. I.B.M. Collection. Heights: 57.5 cm and 54 cm; diameter (bases): 20 cm; weights: 2.44 kg and 2.39 kg. No marks.

Figure 7

CANDELABRUM WITH NIMBUS, Paraguay, late 17th. c. I.B.M.
Collection. Jesuit Mission style. Height: 56.5 cm; width (widest
21.5 cm; weight: 467.78 gr. No marks.

Figure 8

CANDLESCONCE (one of a pair), Paraguay, late 17th. c. I.B.M.
Collection. Jesuit Mission style. Height: 34.5 cm; width (wings):
21.5 cm; weight: 467.78 kg. No marks.

Figure 9

BAPTISMAL SHELL (two views), Peru, late 18th. c. I.B.M. Collection. Depth: 33 cm; width: 42.5 cm; height: 8.5 cm; weight: 1.5 kg. No marks.

Figure 10

A. CROWN, Guatemala, late 18th. or early 19th. c. Museum of New Mexico Collection. For statue of Virgin. Diameter (bottom): 12 cm; diameter (top): 18 cm; height: 8 cm; weight: 233.89 gr. No marks.

B. FILIGREE CROWN, Guatemala, 18th. c. Museum of New Mexico Collection. Diameter (bottom): 2 cm; height (overall): 3.3 cm; weight: 7.09 gr. No marks.

Figure 11

A. CROWN, Colombia, 18th.
c. Museum of New Mexico Collection. For small statue of Virgin. Diameter (bottom): 6.9
cm; height (overall): 12.5 cm;
weight: 141.75 gr. No marks.

B. NIMBUS (halo for holy image), Ecuador, 18th. c. Museum of New Mexico Collection. Diameter: 5.4 cm; weight:
14.18 gr. No marks.

Figure 12

A. INCENSE BOAT AND SPOON, Mexico, c. 1816. Museum of New Mexico Collection. Bought for el Santuario de Esquipulas in Chimayo, New Mexico at the time it was built between 1814 and 1816. Length (boat): 12 cm; width (boat): 8.7 cm; height: 6.5 cm; weight (with spoon): 311.85 gr. No marks.

B. CHRISMATORY (container for holy oils), probably French, late 19th. c. Museum of New Mexico Collection. Made in three sections. Engraved with "O S" for *Oleo Sanctum* (used for confirmation), "S C" for *Sanctum Chrisma* (used for baptism) and "O I" for *Oleo Infirma* (used for the sick). Diameter: 2.5 cm; height: 6.5 cm; weight: 49.61 gr. Small "LF" and illegible mark on bottom.

Figure 13

A. SMALL TRAY (probably an alms dish), Mexico, 1837. Field Collection. Inscribed with "ESTE PLATO LO MANDO HACER EL S.C.D.M.C. LEMUS EL MES D MAYO D 1837." Length: 19.1 cm; width: 12.5 cm; weight: 255.15 gr. Indistinct mark after inscription.

B. RELIQUARY, Mexico, 18th. c. Museum of New Mexico Collection. Length: (overall): 8.5 cm; width: 5.7 cm; thickness: 1.5 cm; weight: 85.05 gr. No marks.

Figure 14

HELMET-SHAPED EWER, Mexico, 1861–62 or 1867–68. Field Collection. Height: 27 cm; diameter (widest point): 21.9 cm; diameter (base): 12.1 cm; weight: 1.31 kg. Marks:

Figure 15

A. COFFEE POT, Mexico, 1823–43. Morley Collection. Diameter (base): 14 cm; height: 25.3 cm; weight: 1.49 kg. Marks:

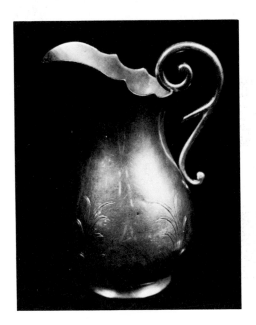

C. TEAPOT, Campeche, Mexico, 18th. c. Morley Collection. Diameter (base): 14.6 cm; height: 19 cm; weight: 730.01 gr. Marks:

B. MILK OR CREAM PITCHER, Guatemala, 18th. c. Morley Collection. Diameter (widest point): 7.6 cm; height: 12.7 cm; weight: 205.54 gr. Marks:

Figure 16

CANDELABRUM, Peru, mid-19th. c. I.B.M. Collection. Style of
Peruvian Independence. Height: 50 cm; diameter (base): 14.5 cm;
width (widest point): 43 cm; weight: 2 kg. No marks.

Figure 17

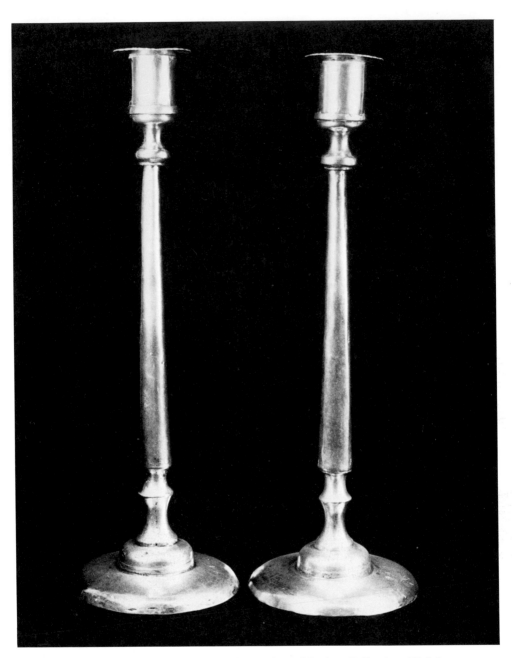

CANDLESTICKS, Guatemala, 17th. c. Morley Collection. Height: 41.2 cm; diameter (base): 13.3 cm; weight (each): 1.33 kg. Marks:

Figure 18

A. CANDLESTICK (one of a pair), Austria, mid-19th. c. Morley Collection. Stamped with Maximilian's emblem, Carlotta's name and silversmith's mark: "V. FUSTER." Diameter (base): 12 cm; height: 22.8 cm; weight (each): 850.5 gr. Marks:

B. CANDLESTICKS, Guatemala, 17th. c. Morley Collection. Diameter (base): 14 cm; height: 31 cm; weight (each): 737.1 gr. Marks:

Figure 19

97

CANDLESTICK (one of a pair), Spain, 17th. c. Museum of New Mexico Collection. Diameter (base): 17 cm; height: 11.5 cm; weight (each): 198.45 gr. Marks:

Figure 20

A. FILIGREE TRAY, Peru, 18th. c. Lyman Collection. Ayacucho "silver lace." Length: 32 cm; width: 25 cm; weight: 574.09 gr. No marks.

B. PLATTER, Mexico, 1791–1818. Morley Collection. Engraved with initials "C.Y." and stamped with owner's mark. Length: 26 cm; depth: 3.2 cm; width: 21 cm; weight: 623.7 gr. Marks:

Figure 21

A. PLATTER, Mexico, 1791–1818. Morley Collection. Probably from shop of master silversmith José María Rodallega (1772–1812). Length: 35.9 cm; width: 23.8 cm; depth: 2.5 cm; weight: 751.28 gr. Marks:

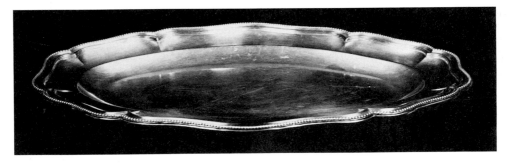

B. PLATTER, Mexico, after 1895. Morley Collection. Length: 45.7 cm; width: 29.2 cm; depth: 2.5 cm; weight: 1.3 kg. Mark:

Figure 22

A. PLATTER, Guatemala, 18th. c. Morley Collection. Length: 31.2 cm; width: 22.8 cm; depth: 2 cm; weight: 793.8 gr. Mark:

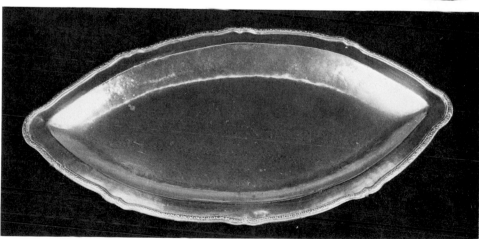

B. FISH PLATTER, Colombia, 19th. c. Lyman Collection. Length: 56.4 cm; width: 29.5 cm; depth: 4.5 cm; weight: 1.01 kg. Mark:

Figure 23

A. SERVING TRAY, Argentina, 18th. or 19th. c. I.B.M. Collection. Diameter: 38.5 cm; depth: 2 cm; weight: 949.73 gr. Marks:

B. BEADED PLATE, Guatemala, 18th. c. Morley Collection. With silversmith's mark "D. ANCULO." Diameter: 22.8 cm; depth: 1.9 cm; weight: 425.25 gr. Marks:

Figure 24

A. FINGER BOWL, Spain, late 17th. c. Museum of New Mexico Collection. Inscribed with a monogram which probably represents "Muñoz." Diameter: 30 cm; depth: 3 cm; weight: 297.68 gr. Official marks illegible.

B. PLAIN PLATE, Mexico, 1773–1778. Morley Collection. Inscribed with "Doña Maria Josepha Calderon y Bermejo" and a ranch brand in the shape of a "Y." Diameter: 23.8 cm; depth: 2 cm; weight: 552.83 gr. Marks:

Figure 25

103

A. FOOTED SALVER, Mexico, 18th. or 19th. c. Field Collection. Probably a genuine old piece which has been stamped with a forged mark later to increase its value. Diameter: 33.3 cm; depth: 3.2 cm; weight: 992.25 gr. Mark:

B. SCALLOPED PLATE, Colombia, 18th. or 19th. c. Lyman Collection. Diameter: 25 cm; depth: 2 cm; weight: 481.95 gr. No marks.

Figure 26

A. SERVING TRAY, Mexico, 18th. c. Field Collection. With monogram composed of "XR" scratched on bottom. Diameter 33.2 cm; depth: 3.5 cm; weight: 1.25 kg. Marks:

B. SALAD PLATE, Mexico, 1791–1818. Morley Collection. Diameter: 16.5 cm; depth: 1.6 cm; weight: 262.24 gr. Marks:

Figure 27

A. SIX-LOBED PLATE,
Mexico, 1823–43. Morley Collection. Diameter: 25 cm;
depth: 2 cm; weight: 510.3 gr.
Marks:

B. EIGHT-LOBED PLATE,
Mexico, 18th. c. Morley Collection. Inscribed with amateurish "CE" on bottom. Diameter: 23.4 cm; depth: 2.5 cm; weight: 963.9 gr. Indistinguishable mark.

Figure 28

A. SALAD PLATE, Mexico, 1823–1843. Morley Collection. With seven lobes. Diameter: 17 cm; depth: 2 cm; weight: 240.98 gr. Marks:

B. SALAD PLATE, Guatemala, 18th. c. Morley Collection. With false (stamped) beading. Diameter: 16.5 cm; depth: 1.5 cm; weight: 283.5 gr. Marks:

Figure 29

A. SALAD PLATE, Guatemala, 18th. c. Morley Collection. With five lobes. Script monogram "MR" on bottom. Diameter: 17.2 cm; depth: 1.5 cm; weight: 212.63 gr. Mark:

B. SALAD PLATE, Mexico, 1823–1843. Morley Collection. Plain edge. Stamped by silversmith Manuel Soriano and silversmith shop. Diameter: 21 cm; depth: 1.5 cm; weight: 396.9 gr. Marks:

Figure 30

A. SIX-LOBED PLAIN PLATE, Mexico, 1791–1818. Field Collection. Stamped by master silversmith Alejandro Antonio de Cañas (1755–1830's) and with owner's mark. Diameter: 24.8 cm; depth: 1.9 cm; weight: 510.3 gr. Marks:

B. FLUTED BOWL, Guatemala, 18th. c. Morley Collection. Letters "LZ" scratched on bottom. Diameter: 15.8 cm; depth: 7.3 cm; weight: 503.21 gr. No marks.

Figure 31

A. LARGE FLUTED BOWL, Mexico, 1791–1818. Field Collection. By master silversmith Antonio Caamaño who served as *veedor* in Mexico City in 1799 and 1801. Diameter: 34.7 cm; depth: 8.6 cm; weight: 1.29 kg. Marks:

B. *BRASERILLO*, probably Mexican, 19th. c. Morley Collection. Inscribed with script initials "GH" on bottom. Length (tray): 21 cm; width (tray): 13.6 cm; diameter (cup): 8.2 cm; height: 12 cm; weight: 368.55 gr. No marks.

Figure 32

A. TWO-HANDLED BOWL, probably Mexican, 18th. c. Morley Collection. Hand inscribed with "Doña Maria Antonia Rocha" on bottom. Diameter: 20.4 cm; height: 11.1 cm; weight: 730.01 gr. No marks.

B. SUGAR BOWL, Peru, mid-19th. c. Museum of New Mexico Collection. Andean style. Diameter (widest point): 7.5 cm; height (overall): 6 cm; weight: 155.93 gr. No marks.

Figure 33

111

A. TUREEN, Bolivia. Probably a 20th. c. reproduction of a colonial piece. Museum of New Mexico Collection. Diameter (with handles): 26.5 cm; height (overall): 21.5 cm; weight: 992.25 gr. No marks.

B. MEDICINE CUP, France, late 19th. c. Museum of New Mexico Collection. Engraved with script monogram "CG" on side. Diameter (top): 6.3 cm; height: 6.4 cm; weight: 56.7 gr. Mark:

Figure 34

A. LARGE BASIN, Mexico, 1823–1843. Morley Collection. With floral design and monogram "F.B." on the bottom, inside. Diameter: 38.1 cm; depth: 8.9 cm; weight: 1.7 kg. Marks:

B. LOBED BOWL, Mexico, late 18th. or early 19th. c. Morley Collection. Monogram "Dn TAV" on bottom. Diameter: 14.7 cm; depth: 6.3 cm; weight: 411.08 gr. Marks:

Figure 35

A. *BRASERILLO*, Mexico, 19th. c. Field Collection. Length (tray) : 21 cm; width (tray) : 12.7 cm; length (bowl) : 12.1 cm; width (bowl) : 9.5 cm; height: 7.6 cm; weight: 368.55 gr. No marks.

B. CUP. Bolivia, 18th. c. Museum of New Mexico Collection. "ANTUNIO DA BALDEVIA" scratched on bottom. Diameter (top) : 6.8 cm; diameter (bottom) : 4.5 cm; height: 7.3 cm; weight: 113.4 gr. No marks.

Figure 36

STEMMED GOBLET, probably Argentine, 18th. c. Museum of
New Mexico Collection. Diameter (base): 6 cm; diameter (cup):
6.2 cm; height: 13 cm; weight: 155.93 gr. Marks:

Figure 37

A. STEMMED GOBLET, Bolivia, probably late 19th. c. Museum of New Mexico Collection. Andean style. Diameter (base): 5.5 cm; diameter (cup): 6.5 cm; height (overall): 13.5 cm; weight: 120.49 gr. No marks.

B. PAIR OF CUPS, Bolivia, modern reproduction of colonial style. Museum of New Mexico Collection. Diameter (tops): 5.3 cm; diameter (bottoms): 3 cm; heights: 6 cm; weight (each): 49.61 gr. No marks.

Figure 38

A. TEACUP, Mexico, after 1895. Lyman Collection. Diameter (top): 7.4 cm; diameter (base): 3.8 cm; height: 7 cm; weight: 77.96 gr. Marks:

B. CUP, Mexico, 1823–1843. Morley Collection. By silversmith Antonio Goderes, documented as active in Mexico City in 1831. Diameter (top): 9.4 cm; height: 8.9 cm; weight: 219.71 gr. Marks:

Figure 39

117

A. TWO-HANDLED CUP, Mexico, late 19th. or early 20th. c.
Lyman Collection. Diameter (top): 6.2 cm; diameter (base): 4.5
cm; height: 7 cm; weight: 120.49 gr. No marks.

B. TEACUP, Mexico, late
19th. or early 20th. c. reproduction. Morley Collection. Diameter (top): 10.1 cm; diameter (base): 5.3 cm; height: 7
cm; weight: 184.28 gr. Forged
marks:

Figure 40

SAHUMADOR (incense burner), Chile, mid-19th. c. I.B.M. Collection. Diameter (base): 12.5 cm; height: 16 cm; weight: 326.03 gr. No marks.

Figure 41

A. MUG WITH SERPENT HANDLE, Mexico, dated 1866. Field
Collection. Inscription: "C. G. A." on one side of handle and
"Jº 20 año de 1866" on the other. Diameter (top): 9.2 cm; diameter (bottom): 7.3 cm; height: 10.5 cm; weight: 411.08 gr. No
marks.

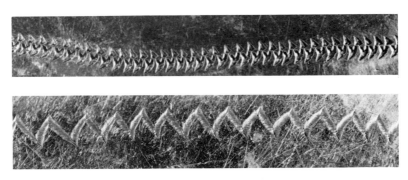

B. Example of *buriladas*.

Figure 42

MUG, Mexico, 17th. c. Field Collection. Diameter (top): 10.2 cm; diameter (bottom): 8.8 cm; height: 12.9 cm; weight: 765.45 gr. No marks.

Figure 43

MUG, Mexico, late 18th. or early 19th. c. Field Collection. Diameter (top): 9.2 cm; diameter (bottom): 5.7 cm; height: 10.5 cm; weight: 396.9 gr. No marks.

Figure 44

A. PAIR OF MUGS, Mexico, probably early 18th. c. Field Collection. Diameter (tops): 9.2 cm; diameter (bottoms): 7 cm; heights: 9.9 cm; weight (each): 297.68 gr. No marks.

B. BEAKER, Mexico, 17th. c. Morley Collection. With initials "M. R." scratched on bottom. Diameter (top): 10.2 cm; diameter (bottom): 7.6 cm; height: 12.1 cm; weight: 304.76 gr. Illegible mark.

Figure 45

A. *MATÉ* CUP, Peru, late 18th. or early 19th. c. I.B.M. Collection. Andean style. Diameter: 8.5 cm; height: 13 cm; weight: 184.28 gr. No marks.

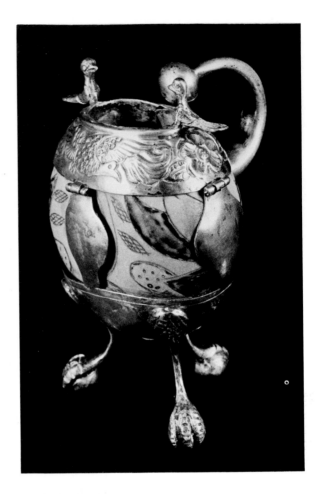

B. *MATÉ* CUP, Bolivia, late 18th. c. I.B.M. Collection. Diameter (saucer): 12.5 cm; height (overall): 11.5 cm; weight: 233.89 gr. No marks.

Figure 46

A. *MATÉ* CUP, Bolivia, 18th. c. Museum of New Mexico Collection. Diameter (widest point): 6.5 cm; diameter (base): 6.5 cm; diameter (rim): 4 cm; height: 9.5 cm; weight: 113.4 gr. No marks.

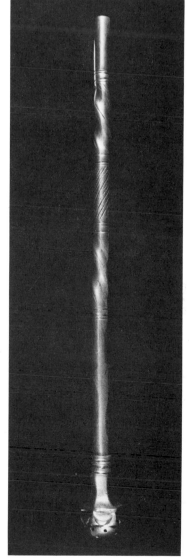

B. *BOMBILLA* (sipping tube), Peru, early 19th. c. I.B.M. Collection. Used with a *maté* cup. Length: 21.5 cm; weight: 49.61 gr. No marks.

Figure 47

A. *MATÉ* CUP, Peru (probably *Limeño*), 18th. or 19th. c. Museum of New Mexico Collection. Diameter (rim): 6.5 cm; height (overall): 10.5 cm; weight: 113.4 gr. No marks.

B. *MATÉ* CUP, Peru, late 18th. or early 19th. c. Lyman Collection. Andean style. Diameter (widest point): 7.5 cm; height (overall): 14 cm; weight: 127.58 gr. No marks.

Figure 48

SERVING FORK AND SPOON, Mexico, 18th. c. Field Collection. Initials "P. D. C." on spoon. Length (fork): 33.4 cm; weight (fork): 191.36 gr.; length (spoon): 30.9 cm; weight (spoon): 141.75 gr. No marks.

Figure 49

A. LADLE, Mexico, 1791–1818. Morley Collection. By master silversmith Antonio Caamaño, *veedor* in Mexico City in 1800, 1801 and 1808. Length: 33 cm; diameter (bowl): 9.5 cm; weight: 283.5 gr. Marks:

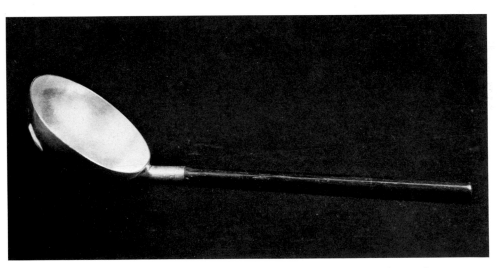

B. LADLE, Mexico, 18th. c. Morley Collection. With black wooden handle. Length: 33.2 cm; diameter (bowl): 11.1 cm; weight: 276.41 gr. No marks.

Figure 50

A. FORKS, Mexico, 18th. and 19th. c. Museum of New Mexico Collection. Average length: 17.3 cm; average weight: 240.98 gr. One mark on back of fork on right:

B. FORKS (two views), Mexico, 18th. c. Museum of New Mexico Collection. With letters "M" and "A" scratched on backs. Average length: 17.3 cm; weight (each): 56.7 gr. No marks.

Figure 51

A. DECORATED SPOONS AND FORKS,
Guatemala, 18th. c. Morley Collection. Twelve
table spoons inscribed with "L. D. T. D."
Length: 18.7 cm; weight (each): 56.7 gr.
Eleven teaspoons and six forks with "T. M. D.
DURÁN" engraved on backs. Length (tea-
spoons): 17.8 cm; weight (each teaspoon):
70.88 gr.; length (forks): 18.7 cm; weight
(each fork): 56.7 gr. No marks.

B. SALT SPOONS, Spain,
17th. c. Museum of New Mexico Collection. Lengths: 10.8
and 10.9 cm; weight (both):
21.26 gr. Marks:

C. UNDECORATED SPOON
AND FORK (matching),
Mexico. 19th. c. Morley Collection. Length: 15.2 cm;
weight (each): 28.35 gr. No
marks.

D. UNDECORATED SPOON
(one of five), Mexico, 19th. c.
Morley Collection. Four with
initials "F. G." scratched on
back and one with "T. G. L."
Average length: 18 cm; average weight: 63.79 gr. No
marks.

Figure 52

A. TRAY FOR CANDLE SNUFFER, Mexico, 1791–1818. Morley Collection. Length: 24.1 cm; width: 10.2 cm; depth: 3.2 cm; weight: 382.73 gr. Marks:

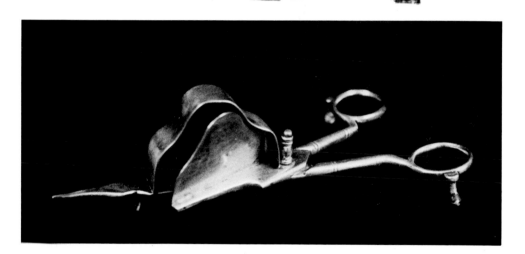

B. CANDLE SNUFFER, Mexico, late 18th. or early 19th. c. Morley Collection. Initials "T M" scratched on bottom. Length: 16.5 cm; width (handles): 6.3 cm; weight: 106.31 gr. No marks.

C. FUNERAL MEMENTO, probably Bolivian, early 19th. c. Museum of New Mexico Collection. Borders on a carved nut inscribed with *"Obceqio a mi padre José Tapía"* and *"Su ijo Benjamín Tapía."* Diameter: 3 cm; length: 6.2 cm; weight: 28.35 gr. No marks.

Figure 53

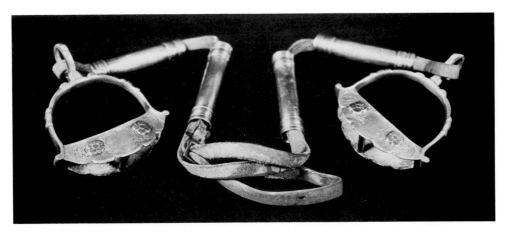

A. STIRRUPS, Argentina, 18th. or early 19th. c. Museum of New Mexico Collection. Silver with gold inlay. Stamped by silversmith "J. OTERO." Height (stirrups): 14 cm; width: 11.4 cm; length (strap guides): 10.2 cm; diameter: 2 cm; weight (with strap): 857.59 gr. Marks:

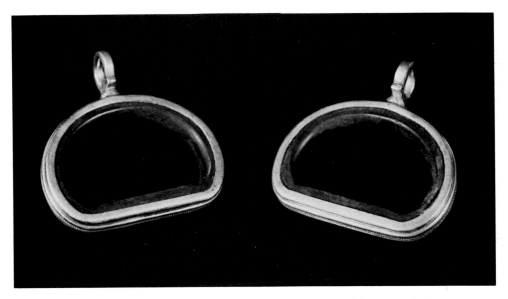

B. STIRRUPS, Argentina, 18th. or early 19th. c. Museum of New Mexico Collection. *Porteño* (Buenos Aires) style. Hollow horn mounted in silver rim. Height (overall): 12.5 cm; width: 12 cm; weight (each): 240.98 gr. No marks.

Figure 54

BELT BUCKLE, Argentina, late 17th. or early 18th. c. Museum of New Mexico Collection. Worn by *gauchos* (cowboys) of the pampas. Three of the eight-*reales* coins dated 1671. Others too worn to distinguish. Diameter (center medallion): 8.5 cm; length (pendants): 6 cm; diameter (coins): 4 cm; weight: 311.85 gr. No marks.

Figure 55

A. *BOLEADORAS* (three *bolas*), Argentina, 18th. c. Museum of New Mexico Collection. Used by *gauchos* (cowboys) of Argentina and neighboring countries instead of a lariat to bring down cattle, horses, wild ostriches and men. Ivory balls with silver mountings attached to twisted rawhide ropes by swivel joints. Length (with ropes): from 96 to 103 cm; diameter (balls): about 5 cm; weight (total): 843.41 gr. No marks.

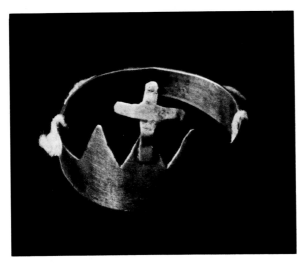

B. CROWN FOR *SANTO NIÑO*, Northern Provincial, Colonial period. Museum of New Mexico Collection. Formerly on seated figure of the Christ Child in chapel near San Juan Pueblo, New Mexico. Diameter: 3.5 cm; height (overall): 2.5 cm; weight: 7.09 gr. No marks.

Figure 56

A. CROWN, rural Colombia, Colonial period. Museum of New Mexico Collection. For life-size statue of Virgin. Diameter: 17 cm; height (overall): 17 cm; weight: 403.99 gr. No marks.

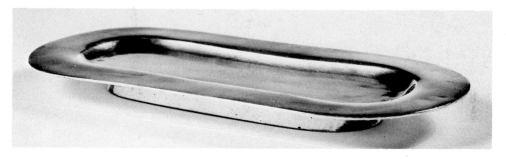

B. CRUET TRAY, Northern Provincial, Colonial period. Field Collection. Length: 21 cm; width: 10.2 cm; weight: 368.55 gr. No marks.

Figure 57

CHALICE, Northern Provincial, Colonial period. Museum of New Mexico Collection. Formerly part of the altar furnishings of a New Mexican colonial church. Height: 22 cm; diameter (base): 14.8 cm; diameter (cup): 7.4 cm; weight: 552.83 gr. No marks.

Figure 58

A. INCENSE BOAT, Northern Provincial, late Colonial period. Field Collection. Initials "R. N." scratched on rim. Height (with hinges): 8.9 cm; length (with handles): 12.7 cm; width (bowl): 9.5 cm; weight: 283.5 gr. No marks.

B. LOCKET (two views), *Norteño*, Colonial period. Museum of New Mexico Collection. Silver mounted nut with religious symbols. Diameter: 2.7 cm; weight: 21.26 gr. No marks.

Figure 59

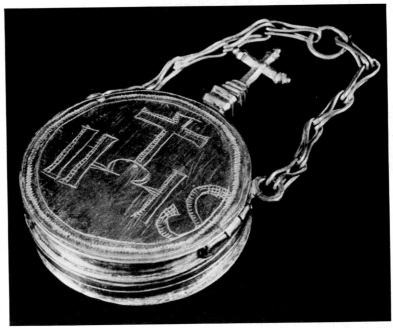

PYX WITH CHAIN (two views), Northern Provincial, Colonial period. Museum of New Mexico Collection. Portable container used to carry a few Hosts to the sick. Diameter (case): 5.5 cm; height (with cross and stem): 8.9 cm; weight: 120.49 gr. No marks.

Figure 60

A. PAIR OF *SAHUMADORES* (incense burners), *Norteño*, Colonial period. Museum of New Mexico Collection. Height: 7 cm; length: 9.8 cm; weight (each): 262.24 gr. No marks.

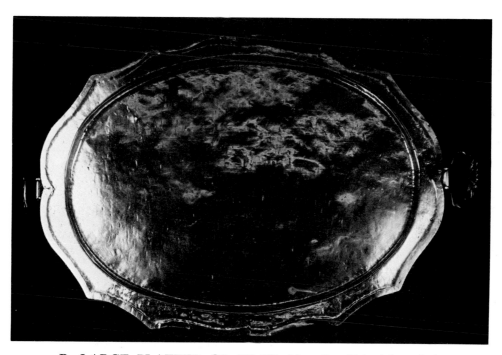

B. LARGE PLATTER OR TRAY, *Norteño*, Colonial period. Lyman Collection. Length: 62 cm; width: 46 cm; depth: 2 cm; weight: 2.35 kg. No marks.

Figure 61

A. LARGE PLATE OR SHALLOW BOWL, *Norteño*, Colonial period. I.B.M. Collection. Script initials "L. C." scratched under rim with small burin. Diameter: 33 cm; depth: 4.2 cm; weight: 1.12 kg. No marks.

B. PLATE OR SHALLOW BOWL, Northern Provincial, Colonial period. Field Collection. Script lettering "R. C. 2" crudely incised on bottom. Diameter: 22.3 cm; depth: 4.1 cm; weight: 396.9 gr. No marks.

Figure 62

A. PLATTER OR LARGE BOWL, Northern Provincial, Colonial period. Field Collection. Length: 39.8 cm; width: 28 cm; depth: 9.2 cm; weight: 1.3 kg. No marks.

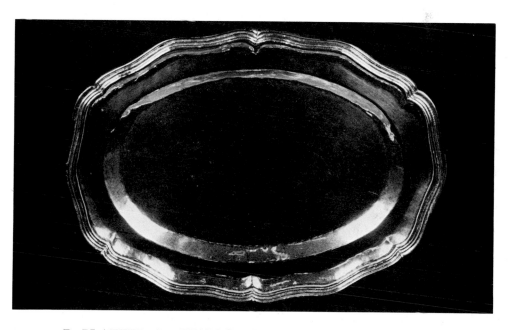

B. PLATTER OR SHALLOW BOWL, rural Colombia, Colonial period. Lyman Collection. Length: 30.5 cm; width: 23 cm; depth: 3.9 cm; weight: 453.6 gr. No marks.

Figure 63

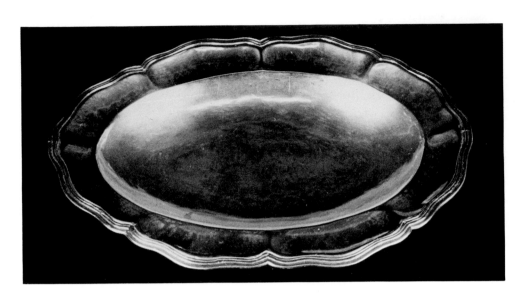

A. SHALLOW DISH, rural Colombia, Colonial period. Lyman Collection. Length: 37 cm; width: 25 cm; depth: 4.5 cm; weight: 687.49 gr. No marks.

B. FLARED PITCHER OR SAUCE DISH, *Norteño*, Colonial period. I.B.M. Collection. With script letters "M. F." on bottom. Diameter (top): 12 cm; diameter (bottom): 6 cm; height: 13 cm; weight: 389.81 gr. No marks.

Figure 64

A. LARGE BOWL, Northern Provincial, Colonial period. Field Collection. Diameter: 43.6 cm; depth: 14.3 cm; weight: 2.3 kg. No marks.

B. GRAVY OR SAUCE BOAT, *Norteño*, Colonial period. I.B.M. Collection. Length (overall): 31 cm; width (widest point): 12.5 cm; height (overall): 14.3 cm; weight: 963.9 gr. No marks.

Figure 65

A. FLUTED BOWL, Northern Provincial, Colonial period. Field Collection. Diameter: 14 cm; depth: 6.4 cm; weight: 340.2 gr. No marks.

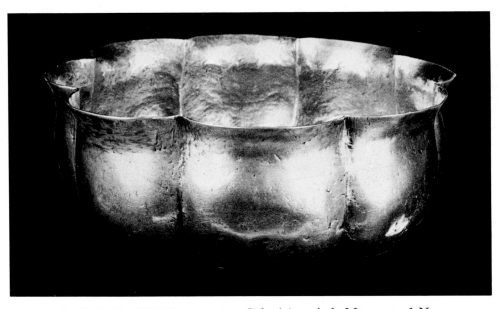

B. LOBED BOWL, *Norteño*, Colonial period. Museum of New Mexico Collection. Diameter: 17.5 cm; height: 7.5 cm; weight: 602.44 gr. No marks.

Figure 66

A. SILVER OLLA, *Norteño*, Colonial period. I.B.M. Collection. With script initial "L" engraved on one wedding ring handle and "T" on the other. Diameter (widest point): 15 cm; height: 15 cm; weight: 637.88 gr. No marks.

B. SMALL BOWL, Northern Provincial, Colonial period. Field Collection. Diameter (rim): 12.7 cm; height: 5.7 cm; weight: 368.55 gr. No marks.

Figure 67

A. FLUTED BOWL, *Norteño*, Colonial period. Museum of New Mexico Collection..Diameter (bowl): 17 cm; diameter (base): 10 cm; depth: 7 cm; weight: 453.6 gr. No marks.

B. STRAIGHT-SIDED BOWL, Northern Provincial, Colonial period. Field Collection. With a bolt and nut through bottom which indicates that it may have originally been a *braserillo* with stemmed cup for live coals attached. Diameter: 12.7 cm; height: 5.4 cm; weight: 368.55 gr. No marks.

Figure 68

A. CUP, rural Colombia, late 19th. c. Lyman Collection. With two patches of solder which may have been applied deliberately to simulate legal marks. Diameter (top): 8 cm; diameter (bottom): 5.5 cm; height: 5.1 cm; weight: 77.96 gr. Mark:

B. CUP, Northern Provincial, Colonial period. Museum of New Mexico Collection. Diameter (top): 8.2 cm; diameter (bottom): 6.5 cm; height: 8 cm; weight: 240.98 gr. No marks.

Figure 69

CUP, rural Bolivia (Lake Titicaca area), after 1820. Museum of New Mexico Collection. Coin set into bottom of
cup from regime of Mariano
Melgarejo, Dictator of Bolivia
from 1820 to 1871. Diameter
(foot): 4.1 cm; diameter (top):
6.8 cm; height: 9 cm; weight:
77.96 gr. No marks.

Figure 70

MUG, Northern Provincial, Colonial period. Field Collection. Diameter (top): 7 cm; diameter (bottom): 5 cm; height: 10.5 cm; weight: 255.15 gr. No marks.

Figure 71

MUG, *Norteño*, Colonial period. Museum of New Mexico Collection. Diameter (top): 8.8 cm; diameter (bottom): 5.6 cm; height: 10.5 cm; weight: 262.24 gr. No marks.

Figure 72

MUG, Northern Provincial, Colonial period. Field Collection. With family name "Pino" inscribed on bottom. Shaped reinforcing plate bolted to inside at top of handle. Diameter (top): 7.6 cm; diameter (bottom): 7 cm; height: 10.8 cm; weight: 396.9 gr. No marks.

Figure 73

MUG, Northern Provincial, Colonial period. Field Collection. Diameter (top): 9.7 cm; diameter (bottom): 6.4 cm; height: 10.5 cm; weight: 368.55 gr. No marks.

Figure 74

MUG, Northern Provincial, Colonial period. Field Collection. Inscribed with "R. N." Diameter (top): 9.2 cm; diameter (bottom):
7 cm; height: 11.4 cm; weight: 368.55 gr. No marks.

Figure 75

HORN MUG, *Norteño*, Colonial period. Museum of New Mexico
Collection. Diameter (top): 9 cm; diameter (bottom): 6.8 cm;
height: 13 cm; weight: 219.71 gr. No marks.

Figure 76

STEMMED GOBLET, Northern Provincial, Colonial period. Field
Collection. Diameter (top): 7.3 cm; diameter (base): 5 cm; height:
13.5 cm; weight: 311.85 gr. No marks.

Figure 77

SILVER CARAFE, Northern Provincial, Colonial period. Morley Collection. Diameter (widest point): 10.2 cm; height: 21.5 cm; weight: 375.64 gr. No marks.

Figure 78

A. *TABAQUERA* WITH
CHAIN, probably made in the
United States, late 19th. c. Mu-
seum of New Mexico Collec-
tion. With the name "JOSEFA
VALDES" and "N. M." on lid.
Height: 6.5 cm; width: 4 cm;
weight: 85.05 gr. No marks.

B. *TABAQUERA*, Northern
Provincial, dated 1887. Field
Collection. Inscribed with
"Nov. 15th, 1887 M. Mon-
toya." Height: 7.6 cm; width:
5 cm; weight: 170.1 gr. No
marks.

C. *TABAQUERA*, Northern
Provincial, Colonial period.
Field Collection. Script initials
"V. B." scratched on bottom.
Height: 5.7 cm; width: 3.8 cm;
weight: 85.05 gr. No marks.

Figure 79

A. PECTORAL. San Blas Islands, early 19th. c. Museum of New Mexico Collection. Decorative breast piece worn by the Indians. Twenty-six two-*reales* coins mint marked in Mexico between 1772 and 1807. One from San Blas Islands, off the coast of Panama, dated 1808. Length: 19 cm; weight: 191.36 gr. No marks.

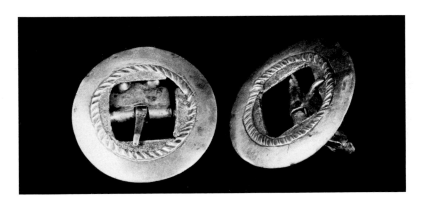

B. HARNESS BUCKLES, rural Mexico, Colonial period. Museum of New Mexico Collection. Clamps were riveted to rawhide straps. Diameter: 6 cm; weight (each): 28.35 gr. No marks.

C. *CONCHA*, rural Mexico, Colonial period. Museum of New Mexico Collection. Decoration for bridle or harness. Diameter: 5.3 cm; weight: 21.26 gr. No marks.

Figure 80

BIBLIOGRAPHY

Abeledo, A. Enrique. "Argentine Folk Arts," *Américas,* Vol. 21, No. 5 (May, 1969), 34–39.

Abert, J. W. *Examinations of New Mexico in the Years 1846–47.* House Executive Documents, Thirtieth Congress, First Session, Doc. 41. Washington: Government Printing Office, 1848.

Adair, John. *The Navajo and Pueblo Silversmiths.* Norman: University of Oklahoma Press, 1944.

Ahlborn, Richard E. *Domestic Silver in Colonial Mexico and Comments on Peru.* 1968 Winterthur Conference Report, pp. 32–46. Winterthur, Delaware: Henry Francis du Pont Museum, 1969.

———. *The Ecclesiastical Silver of Colonial Mexico.* 1968 Winterthur Conference Report, pp. 19–31. Winterthur, Delaware: Henry Francis du Pont Museum, 1969.

———. *Three Centuries of Peruvian Silver.* Exhibition Catalogue, *Three Centuries of Peruvian Silver,* pp. 33–36. Washington: Smithsonian Institution; New York: Metropolitan Museum of Art, 1968.

Allison, W. H. H. (Ralph Emerson Twitchell, ed.). "Colonel Francisco Perea," *Old Santa Fe,* I, No. 4 (April, 1914), 212–218.

Anderson, Lawrence. *The Art of the Silversmith in Mexico 1519–1936,* Vols. I & II. New York: Oxford University Press, 1941.

Bargalló, Modesto. *La minería y la metalurgia en la America Española durante la época colonial.* Mexico-Buenos Aires: Fondo de Cultura and Económica, 1955.

Berlin, Heinrich. *Artistas y artesanos coloniales de Guatemala.* Cuadernos de Antropológia, Instituto de Investigaciones Históricas, Guatemala: Facultad de Humanidades, Departamento de Publicaciones, Universidad de San Carlos, 4–9 de 1965.

Blasi Brambilla, Alberto. "The Three Marías," *Américas,* Vol. 21, No. 7 (July, 1969), 33–39.

Boyd, E. "Colonial Silver from Latin America," *El Palacio,* Vol. 69/2 (1962), 119–123.

Chávez, Fray Angélico. *Origins of New Mexico Families.* Santa Fe, New Mexico: The Historical Society of New Mexico, 1954.

Chittenden, Hiram Martin. *The American Fur Trade of the Far West,* 3 Vols. New York: Francis P. Harper, 1902.

Coues, Elliott (ed. & annot.) *The Expeditions of Zebulon Montgomery Pike,* 3 Vols. New York: Francis P. Harper, 1895.

Dominguez, Fray Francisco Anastasio (trans., Adams, E. & Chávez, Fray A.). *The Missions of New Mexico, 1776.* Albuquerque: University of New Mexico Press, 1956.

Drew, Laurel E. ''Henrika (Busch) Huning,'' Paper 29/Y, Special Collections, Zimmerman Library, University of New Mexico, 1963. (Typescript.)

Emory, W. H. *Lieutenant Emory Reports.* Albuquerque: University of New Mexico Press, 1951.

Ensko, Stephen Guernsey Cook. *American Silversmiths and Their Marks.* New York: Robert Ensko, Inc., Gold and Silversmiths, 1948.

Espinosa, Gilberto. ''A Guide to New Mexico Genealogical Study,'' Special Collections, Zimmerman Library, University of New Mexico, n.d. (Typescript.)

Espinosa, T. Manuel (trans.). *First Expedition of de Vargas Into New Mexico, 1692.* Albuquerque: University of New Mexico Press, 1940.

Faniel, Stéphane (ed.). *French Art of the 18th Century.* New York: Simon & Shuster, 1957.

Fosque, Edwin J. *Taxco, Mexico's Silver City.* Dallas, Texas: Southern Methodist University Press, 1947.

Hallenbeck, Cleve. *Land of the Conquistadores.* Caldwell, Idaho: The Caxton Printers, Ltd., 1950.

Hammond, George P. *Don Juan de Oñate and the Founding of New Mexico.* Santa Fe, New Mexico: El Palacio Press, 1927.

———— & Agapito Rey. *Don Juan de Oñate, Colonizer of New Mexico, 1598–1628,* Vol. I. Albuquerque: University of New Mexico Press, 1953.

Harcourt, Raoul d'. *L' ar̄genterie peruvienne a L' epoque colonial.* Paris: Editions Albert Morance, 1927.

Haring, C. H. *The Spanish Empire in America.* New York: Oxford University Press, 1947.

Harth-Terre, Emilio. *Silver and Silversmiths of Peru.* Exhibition Catalogue, *Three Centuries of Peruvian Silver,* pp. 25–31. Washington: Smithsonian Institution; New York: Metropolitan Museum of Art, 1968.

Hodge, F. W. *Bibliography of Fray Alonso de Benevides.* Indian Notes and Monographs, Vol. II. New York: Museum of the American Indian, Heye Foundation, 1919–1920.

————, George P. Hammond & Agapito Rey (eds.). *Fray Alonso de Benevides Revised Memorial of 1634.* Albuquerque: University of New Mexico Press, 1945.

Horgan, Paul. *The Great River,* Vols. I & II. New York: Rinehart & Co., 1954.

Hunt, Walter Bernard. *Indian Silversmithing.* Milwaukee, Wisconsin: Bruce Publishing Co., 1952.

Johnson, Ada Marshall. *Hispanic Silverwork.* New York: Hispanic Society of America, Catalogue Series, 1944.

Keleher, William A. *Turmoil in New Mexico, 1846–1868.* Santa Fe, New Mexico: Rydal Press, 1952.

Kubler, George. *Time's Reflection and Colonial Art.* 1968 Winterthur Conference Report, pp. 7–18. Winterthur, Delaware: Henry Francis du Pont Museum, 1969.

Larco Hoyle, Constante. *Silver Trainings [read Trappings] of the Peruvian Horse Harness.* Exhibition Catalogue, *Three Centuries of Peruvian Silver,* pp. 37–39. Washington: Smithsonian Institution; New York: Metropolitan Museum of Art, 1968.

Laughlin, Ruth. *Caballeros.* Caldwell, Idaho: The Caxton Printers, Ltd., 1945.

Maldonado-Koerdell, Manuel. "Silver and Gold in Mexico's Destiny," *Artes de México,* No. 112 (1968), 11–12.

Marquez-Miranda, Fernando. *Los artífices de la platería en Buenos Aires colonial.* Facultad de Filosofía y Letras, Publicaciones del Instituto de Investigaciones y Históricas, Numero LXII. Buenos Aires: Imprenta de la Universidad, 1933.

Mera, Harry P. *Indian Silverwork in the Southwest.* Globe, Arizona: Dale Stuart King, 1959.

Moorehead, Max L. *New Mexico's Royal Road, Trade and Travel on the Chihuahua Trail.* Norman: University of Oklahoma Press, 1954.

Moses, Elisabeth. Exhibition Catalogue, *Three Centuries of European and Domestic Silver.* San Francisco, California: M. H. de Young Memorial Museum, October, 1938.

Motten, Clement G. *Mexican Silver and the Enlightenment.* Philadelphia: University of Pennsylvania Press, 1950.

Oberti, Frederico. "Platería," *Arte popular y artesanías tradicionales de la Argentina,* E 6 serie del siglo y medio (1964), 24–27.

Obregón, Gonzalo. "Corrientes estilísticas en la orfebrería mexicana," *Artes de México,* No. 112 (1968), 24–29.

Oman, C. C. *English Domestic Silver.* London: A. & C. Black, Ltd., 1934.

Ortiz Family Papers, Documents Nos. 2 & 3. Santa Fe, New Mexico: State Records & Archives.

Picón-Sales, Mariano. *De la conquista a la independencia/tres siglos de cultura Hispanamericana.* Second edition. México-Buenos Aires: Fondo de Cultura Económica, 1950.

Pino, Barriero, Escudero. (trans., Carroll & Haggard). *Three New Mexico Chronicles.* Albuquerque, New Mexico: The Quivira Society, 1950.

Pizano y Saucedo, Carlos. *Platería, siglo XX,* Jalisco en el Arte Series. Guadalajara, México: Planeación y Promoción, S. A., 1960.

Quinn, R. M. *The Spanish Colonial Style,* Exhibition Catalogue, *The Colonial Arts of Latin America.* Tucson, Arizona: Tucson Art Center, 1/8–2/12, 1966.

Rafael, Lorenzo. "The Silversmith's Trade in Mexico," *Artes de México,* No. 112 (1968), 77–83.

Romero de Terreros, Manuel. *Arte colonial,* Vol. I. México, D. F.: Imprenta de J. Ballesca, 1916.

Romero de Terreros y Vinent, Manuel. *Las artes industriales en la Nueva España.* México, D. F.: Librería de Pedro Robredo, 1923.

Samayoa Guevara, Hector Umberto. "El gremio de plateros de la Ciudad de Guatemala y sus ordenanzas, 1524–1821." *Antropología e historia de Guatemala,* Vol. IX, No. 1 (January, 1957), 19–44.

———. *Los gremios de artesanos en la Ciudad de Guatemala,* (1524–1821). Guatemala: editorial Universitaria, 1962.

Scholes, France V. *The Church and State in New Mexico, 1610–1650.* Albuquerque: University of New Mexico Press, 1937.

———. *Troublous Times in New Mexico, 1659–1670.* Albuquerque: University of New Mexico Press, 1942.

———, and Eleanor B. Adams, "Inventories of Church Furnishings in Some of the New Mexican Missions, 1672." *Dargan Historical Essays,* ed. William M. Dabney and Josiah C. Russell. Univ. of New Mexico Publications in History, No. 4, Albuquerque, 1952.

Schuetz, Mardith K., "Historic Background of the Mission San Antonio de Valero." State Building Commission

Archeological Program, Report No. 1, Nov. 1966. Austin, Texas.

Smith, Robert C. *The Art of Portugal, 1500-1800*. New York: Meredith Press, 1968.

Stephens, John Lloyd. *Incidents of Travel in Central America, Chiapas, and Yucatan,* 2 Vols. New York: Harper & Brothers, 1841.

Sunder, John E. (ed.), (collected by Clyde and Mae Porter). *Matt Field on the Santa Fe Trail*. Norman: University of Oklahoma Press, 1960.

Taullard, Alfredo. *Platería sudamericana*. Buenos Aires: Peuser, Ltda., 1941.

Torre Revello, José. *El gremio de plateros en las Indies Occidentales*. Facultad de Filosofía y Letras, Publicaciones del Instituto de Investigaciones Históricas, Numero LVI. Buenos Aires: Imprenta de la Universidad, 1932.

———. *La orfebrería colonial en Hispanoamérica y particularamente en Buenos Aires*. Buenos Aires: Editorial Huarpes, S. A., 1945.

Toussaint, Manuel. *Arte colonial de México*. Mexico, D. F.: Imprenta Universitaria, 1962.

Twitchell, Ralph Emerson. *The Leading Facts of New Mexican History,* 5 Vols. Cedar Rapids, Iowa: The Torch Press, 1911–17.

——— (ed.). *The Spanish Archives of New Mexico,* Vol. I. Cedar Rapids, Iowa: The Torch Press, 1914.

Ugarte Eléspuru, Juan Manuel. *Peruvian Culture During the Viceroyalty*. Exhibition Catalogue, *Three Centuries of Peruvian Silver,* pp. 19–23. Washington: Smithsonian Institution; New York: Metropolitan Museum of Art, 1968.

Ugarteche, Carlos Neuhaus. *Treasures of Peruvian Antiquity*. Exhibition Catalogue, *Three Centuries of Peruvian Silver,* pp. 15–17. Washington: Smithsonian Institution; New York: Metropolitan Museum of Art, 1968.

Valle-Arizpe, D. Artemio de. "Ladrones sacrilegos y plateros inquisitoriados," *Arte y Plata* (October, 1945), 13–16.

———. *Notas de platería*. México, D. F.: Editorial Polis, 1941.

Wenham, Edward. *The Practical Book of American Silver*. Philadelphia and New York: J. B. Lippencott Company, 1949.

———. "Spanish American Silver in New Mexico," *International Studio,* Vol. 99 (January, 1931), 31–33.

Wilgus, Curtis A. *Historical Atlas of Latin America*. New York: Cooper Square Publishers, Inc., 1967.

Woodward, Arthur. *A Brief History of Navajo Silversmithing*. Flagstaff: Northern Arizona Society of Science and Art, 1946.

Wyler, Seymour B. *The Book of Old Silver*. New York: Crown Publishers, 1937.

APPENDICES

APPENDIX I

CATALOGUE

MUSEUM OF NEW MEXICO COLLECTION

Note: The Museum of New Mexico Collection, the International Business Machines Collection, the Lyman Collection and the Morley Collection all belong to the Museum of New Mexico. All are housed in the International Museum of Folk art (a division of the Museum) except the Morley, which is in the Palace of the Governors in Santa Fe, New Mexico.

PAIR OF CANDLESTICKS (Fig. 6), Mexico, dated 1729. Inscription on triangular bases: *"SON DE LA ARCHCOERA DADE S SMO/DE LA YGLESIA DE ESTA NUEBA BERA CRUZ/ANO DE 1729."* Heights: 55 cm; widths (bases): 17 cm; weights: 3.777 kg. and 3.904 kg. Stamped with a *Mundos y Mares* (hallmark of quality), eagle (tax mark) and artisan's mark "LIN" over "CR" (unidentified). Loaned by Fred Harvey Foundation.

PAIR OF CANDLESTICKS (Fig. 20), Spain, 17th c. Diameter (base): 17 cm; height: 11.5 cm; weight (each): 198.45 gr. Stamped with tiny lion with front paw lifted (unidentified) and another mark too faint to identify.

CROWN (Fig. 11-A), Guatemala, late 18th or early 19th c. For large statue of Virgin. Diameter (bottom): 12 cm; diameter (top): 18 cm; height: 8 cm; weight: 233.89 gr. No marks.

CROWN (Fig. 12-A), Colombia, 18th c. For small statue of Virgin. Diameter (bottom): 6.9 cm; height (overall): 12.5 cm; weight: 141.75 gr. No marks.

CROWN (not illustrated), Guatemala, 19th c. With six rays on spiral springs. Diameter (bottom): 7 cm; diameter (widest point): 12 cm; height (overall): 13 cm; weight: 198.45 gr. No marks. Loaned by Mrs. Edith Ricketson.

CROWN (Fig. 57-A), rural Colombia, Colonial period. For life-size statue of Virgin. Diameter: 17 cm; height (overall): 17 cm; weight: 403.99 gr. No marks.

CROWN FOR *SANTO NINO* (Fig. 56-B), Northern provincial, Colonial period. From chapel near San Juan

Pueblo, New Mexico. Diameter: 3.5 cm; height (overall): 2.5 cm; weight: 709 gr. No marks. Gift of Father Burke.

FILIGREE CROWN (Fig. 11-B), Guatemala, 18th c. Originally on polychrome statuette of the Virgin given to the museum by Dr. Sylvanus Griswold Morley. Diameter (bottom): 2 cm; height (overall): 3.3 cm; weight: 7.09 gr. No marks.

NIMBUS (Fig. 12-B), Ecuador, 18th c. Halo for small statue. Originally attached to back of head with a short prong. Diameter: 5.4 cm; weight: 14.18 gr. No marks.

CHRISMATORY (Fig. 13-B), probably French, late 19th c. Container for holy oils made in three sections. Engraved with "O S" *(Oleo Sanctum),* "S C" *(Sanctum Chrisma)* and "O I" *(Oleo Infirma).* Diameter: 2.5 cm; height: 6.5 cm; weight: 49.61 gr. Small "LF" and illegible mark (may be head of Hermes.

CHRISMATORY (not illustrated), Spain, 18th or 19th c. Two sections with lid. Engraved with "I" *(Infirmorum)* and "C" (Catechumen). Diameter: 2.5 cm; height: 4.7 cm; weight: 42.53 gr. Tiny punch mark "IX" inside lid (unidentified).

INCENSE BOAT AND SPOON (Fig. 13-A), Mexico, about 1816. Bought for the Santuario de Esquipulas in el Potrero de Chimayo, New Mexico when it was built, 1814–1816. Length (boat): 12 cm; width (boat): 8.7 cm; height: 6.5 cm; weight (with spoon): 311.85 gr. No marks. Gift of Miss M. V. Conkey.

RELIQUARY (Fig. 14-B), Mexico, 18th c. From maternal family of Mauricio Sánchez, Albuquerque, New Mexico. Length (overall): 8.5 cm; width: 5.7 cm; thickness: 1.5 cm; weight: 85.05 gr. No marks.

PYX WITH CHAIN (Fig. 60), Northern Provincial, Colonial period. Diameter (case): 5.5 cm; length (with cross and stem): 8.9 cm; weight: 120.49 gr. No marks. Loaned by Mr. John Sandoval.

LOCKET (Fig. 59-B), *Norteño,* Colonial period. Nut with silver mounting and decorations. Diameter: 2.7 cm; weight: 21.26 gr. No marks.

PAIR OF *SAHUMADORES* (Fig. 61-A), *Norteño,* Colonial period. Height: 7 cm; length: 9.8 cm; weight (each): 262.24 gr. Collected by Miss Florence Dibell Bartlett. No marks.

MEMENTO (Fig. 53-C), probably Bolivian, early 19th c. With *"Obseqio mi padre José Tapía"* and *"Su ijo Benjamín Tapía"* inscribed on borders of carved nut. Diameter: 3 cm; length: 6.2 cm; weight: 28.35 gr. No marks.

CHALICE (Fig. 58), Northern Provincial, Colonial period. Formerly part of furnishings of the parish church of Santa Fe, New Mexico. Height: 22 cm; diameter (base): 14.8 cm; diameter (cup): 7.4 cm; weight: 552.83 gr. No marks.

TABAQUERA (not illustrated), Northern Provincial, Colonial period. Chain lost. Length: 5.4 cm; width: 4.3 cm; weight: 56.7 gr. No marks. Gift of Miss M. V. Conkey.

TABAQUERA WITH CHAIN (Fig. 79-A), probably made in the United States, late 19th c., of German silver and decorated in New Mexico. Letters "JOSEFA VALDES" and "N. M." on lid stamped individually like those used during territorial period to mark gun plates, harness brass and other pieces of personal property. Height: 6.5 cm; width: 4 cm; weight: 85.05 gr. No marks.

SNUFF BOX (not illustrated), American, early 20th c. Length: 8.5 cm; height: 3 cm; width: 3.5 cm;

weight: 85.05 gr. Marked with "GORMAN" and anchor under front lip. Gift of Miss M. V. Conkey.

FINGER BOWL (Fig. 25-A), Spain, late 17th c. With monogram that probably represents "Muñoz." Diameter: 30 cm; depth: 3 cm; weight: 297.68 gr. Marks illegible. Gift of Victor Hammer.

SUGAR BOWL (Fig. 33-B), Peru, mid-19th c. Andean style. Diameter (widest point): 7.5 cm; height (overall): 6 cm; weight: 155.93 gr. No marks. Collected for the museum by Miss Florence Dibell Bartlett.

TUREEN (Fig. 34-A), Bolivia, early 20th c. Probably a reproduction of colonial piece. Diameter (with handles): 26.5 cm; height (overall): 21.5 cm; weight: 992.25 gr. No marks.

PLATTER (not illustrated), Spain, 18th c. Length: 31.5 cm; width: 19.3 cm; depth: 2 cm; weight: 333.11 gr. Stamped with castle, crown (probably hallmarks of quality) and "M" (verified by Ortega of Seville as mark of Martínez family who worked in Madrid in 18th c.).

ROUND TRAY (not illustrated), Bolivia, early 20th c. Reproduction of a colonial piece. Hinged handles with stylized leaf and grape design. Diameter: 28 cm; depth: 2 cm; weight: 368.55 gr. No marks. Loaned from David Thornburg collection.

LARGE PLATE (not illustrated), Spain, 18th c. Diameter: 29.7 cm; depth: 3.3 cm; weight: 588.26 gr. Stamped with castle, crown (probably hallmarks of quality) and number "11."

LOBED BOWL (Fig. 66-B), *Norteño*, Colonial period. Squash form. Diameter: 17.5 cm; height: 7.5 cm; weight: 602.44 gr. No marks. Gift of Miss Mary Cabot Wheelwright.

FLUTED BOWL (Fig. 68-A), *Norteño*, Colonial period. With scalloped rim

and inverted pedestal base. Diameter (bowl): 17 cm; diameter (base): 10 cm; depth: 7 cm; weight: 453.6 gr. Gift of Mary Cabot Wheelwright. No marks.

STEMMED GOBLET (Fig. 37), probably Argentine, 18th c. Diameter (base): 6 cm; diameter (cup): 6.2 cm; height: 13 cm; weight: 155.93 gr. Stamped with "AA" (unidentified) and number with only first two digits, "84—," legible.

STEMMED GOBLET (Fig. 38-A), Bolivia, probably late 19th c. Andean style. Diameter (base): 5.5 cm; diameter (cup): 6.5 cm; height (overall): 13.5 cm; weight: 120.49 gr. No marks. Gift of Miss Mary Cabot Wheelwright.

MEDICINE CUP (Fig. 34-B), France, late 19th c. Engraved with script monogram "CG" on side. Diameter (top): 6.3 cm; height: 6.4 cm; weight: 56.7 gr. Stamped with caduceus on bottom. Gift of Miss M. V. Conkey.

CUP (Fig. 69-B), Northern Provincial, Colonial period. Handle repaired by being forced into a triangular shape. Diameter (top): 8.2 cm; diameter (bottom): 6.5 cm; height: 8 cm; weight: 240.98 gr. No marks. Gift of Miss M. V. Conkey.

CUP (Fig. 70), rural Bolivia (Lake Titicaca area), after 1820. With coin from regime of Mariano Melgarejo, dictator of Bolivia from 1820–1871, set in bottom. Diameter (foot): 4.1 cm; diameter (top): 6.8 cm; height: 9 cm; weight: 77.96 gr. No marks. Loaned from David Thornburg collection.

CUP (not illustrated), Bolivia, early 20th c. Reproduction of a colonial piece. Diameter (bottom): 6 cm; diameter (top): 10 cm; height: 12 cm; weight: 240.98 gr. No marks. Loaned from David Thornburg collection.

CUP (Fig. 36-B), Bolivia, 18th c. "ANTUNIO DA BALDEVIA" scratched on bottom. Diameter (top): 6.8 cm;

165

diameter (bottom): 4.5 cm; height: 7.3 cm; weight: 113.4 gr. No marks. Loaned from David Thornburg collection.

PAIR OF CUPS (Fig. 38-B), Bolivia, modern reproduction of colonial style. Diameter (tops): 5.3 cm; diameter (bottoms): 3 cm; heights: 6 cm; weight (each): 49.61 gr. No marks. Loaned from David Thornburg collection.

SET OF FIVE CUPS (not illustrated), Bolivia, early 20th c. Reproductions of colonial style. Graduated sizes. Diameter (tops): from 3.5 cm to 7 cm; diameter (bottoms): from 2.3 cm to 4.1 cm; heights: from 4 cm to 8 cm; weights: from 21.26 to 120.49 gr. No marks. Loaned from David Thornburg collection.

MATE CUP (Fig. 47-A), Bolivia, 18th c. With squash handle. Diameter (widest point): 6.5 cm; diameter (base): 6.5 cm; diameter (rim): 4 cm; height: 9.5 cm; weight: 113.4 gr. No marks. Gift of Miss Mary Cabot Wheelwright.

MATE CUP (Fig. 48-A), Peru (probably *Limeño*), 18th or 19th c. Ovoid nut with silver base, handles and lid. Diameter (rim): 6.5 cm; height (overall): 10.5 cm; weight: 113.4 gr. No marks. Gift of Miss Mary Cabot Wheelwright.

MUG (Fig. 72), *Norteño*, Colonial period. With fishtail handle. Diameter (top): 8.8 cm; diameter (bottom): 5.6 cm; height: 10.5 cm; weight: 262.24 gr. No marks. Gift of Miss M. V. Conkey.

MUG (not illustrated), Mexico, late 18th c. Tulip shaped with flange base. Diameter (top): 9 cm; diameter (bottom): 5.4 cm; height: 11.2 cm; weight: 389.81 gr. No marks. Gift of Miss M. V. Conkey.

HORN MUG (Fig. 76), *Norteño*, Colonial period. Diameter (top): 9 cm; diameter (bottom): 6.8 cm; height: 13 cm; weight: 219.71 gr. No marks. Loaned from David Thornburg collection.

TWO FORKS (Fig. 51-B), Mexico, 18th c. With letters "M" and "A" scratched on backs. Average length: 17.3 cm; weight (each): 56.7 gr. No marks.

FOUR FORKS (Fig. 51-A), Mexico, 18th and 19th c. Found by the late John Wallace when utility trench was dug in front of Governor's Palace, Santa Fe, New Mexico, Average length: 17.3 cm; average weight: 240.98 gr. One stamped with "Z" with a superimposed "o" (unidentified).

ONE UNDECORATED TEASPOON (not illustrated), Mexico, 1823–1843. With "Chabes" scratched on back. Stamped with eagle (tax mark), "M" with "o" (Mexico City) and "BTON" (genuine marks of Chief Assayer Cayetano Buitrón) and name of either José María Torre or Mariano de la Torre, both silversmiths who worked during Buitrón's term in office. Length: 19 cm; weight: 113.4 gr.

ONE DECORATED TEASPOON (similar to Fig. 52-A), Guatemala, 18th c. With "Modesto Barrera" engraved on back. Length: 15 cm; weight: 28.35 gr. No marks.

TWO SALT SPOONS (Fig. 52-B), Spain, 17th c. Lengths: 10.8 cm; and 10.9 cm; weight (together): 21.26 gr. Stamped with rampant lion (probably hallmark of quality), "ALVARES" with "M" above and "R. MARTOS" with "72" above.

BELT BUCKLE (Fig. 55), Argentina, late 17th or early 18th c. Worn by *gauchos* of the pampas. Three of the eight-*reales* coins dated 1671. Others indistinguishable. Diameter (center medallion): 8.5 cm; length (pendants): 6 cm; diameter (coins): 4 cm; weight: 311.85 gr. No marks.

PECTORAL (Fig. 80-A), San Blas

Islands, early 19th c. Twenty-six two-*reales* coins mint marked in Mexico between 1772 and 1807. One from San Blas Islands, off the coast of Panama, dated 1808. Length: 19 cm; weight: 191.36 gr. No marks.

STIRRUPS (Fig. 54-A), Argentina, 18th or early 19th c. Silver with gold inlay. Height (stirrups): 14 cm; width: 11.4 cm; length (strap guides): 10.2 cm; diameter: 2 cm; weight (with strap): 857.59 gr. Stamped by silversmith "J. OTERO" and the number "900."

STIRRUPS (Fig. 54-B). Argentina, 18th or early 19th c. *Porteño* (Buenos Aires) style. Hollow horn mounted in silver. Height (overall): 12.5 cm; width: 12 cm; weight (each): 240.98 gr. No marks. Loaned from David Thornburg collection.

BOLEADORAS (Fig. 56-A), Argentina, 18th c. Three ivory balls *(bolas)* with silver mountings attached to twisted rawhide ropes by swivel joints. Length (with ropes): from 96 cm to 103 cm; diameter (balls): about 5 cm; weight (total): 843.41 gr. No marks.

HARNESS BUCKLES (Fig. 80-B), rural Mexico, Colonial period. Clamps were riveted to rawhide straps. Diameter: 6 cm; weight (each): 28.35 gr. No marks.

CONCHA (Fig. 80-C), rural Mexico, Colonial period. Decoration for bridle or harness. Diameter: 5.3 cm; weight: 21.26 gr. No marks.

CATALOGUE

MORLEY COLLECTION

MUSEUM OF NEW MEXICO, SANTA FE

*COFFEE POT (Fig. 16-A), Mexico, 1823–43. Diameter (base): 14 cm; height: 25.3 cm; weight: 1.49 kg. Stamped with eagle (tax mark), "M" with "o" (Mexico City) and "BTON" (genuine marks of Chief Assayer Cayetano Buitrón).

*TEAPOT (Fig. 16-C), Campeche, Mexico, 18th c. Diameter (base): 14.6 cm; height: 19 cm; weight: 730.01 gr. Stamped with crown, Santiago over two peaks (both stand for tax and quality) and monogram "RNB."

*MILK OR CREAM PITCHER (Fig. 16-B), Guatemala, 18th c. Diameter (widest point): 7.6 cm; height: 12.7 cm; weight: 205.54 gr. Stamped with crown and Santiago over two peaks (both stand for tax and quality).

*PAIR OF CANDLESTICKS (Fig. 18), Guatemala, 17th c. Height: 41.2 cm; diameter (base): 13.3 cm; weight (each): 1.332 kg. Stamped with crown and lion over two peaks (both stand for tax and quality).

*PAIR OF CANDLESTICKS (Fig. 19-A), Austria, mid-19th c. Diameter (base): 12 cm; height: 22.8 cm; weight (each): 850.5 gr. Stamped with Maximilian's emblem ("M" surmounted by indistinguishable object), Carlotta's name and silversmith's mark "V. FUSTER."

PAIR OF CANDLESTICKS (Fig. 19-B), Guatemala, 17th c. Diameter (base): 14 cm; height: 31 cm; weight (each): 737.1 gr. Stamped with two crowns and lion over two peaks (all stand for tax and quality).

FOUR CANDLESCONCES (not illustrated), Mexico, 1791–1818.

Originally attached to silver chandelier. Diameter (saucer of *bobêche*): 12.7 cm; height (overall): 16.5 cm; weight (each): 524.48 gr. Stamped with eagle (tax mark), "M" crowned (Mexico City) and "FCDA" (the genuine marks of Chief Assayer Antonio Forcada y La Plaza) and name of either Francisco Villegas, who was examined in Mexico City in 1792, or master silversmith José Antonio Villegas, examined in 1786.

*PLATTER (Fig. 21-B), Mexico, 1791–1818. Engraved with initials "C.Y." Length: 26 cm; width: 21 cm; depth: 3.2 cm; weight: 623.7 gr. Stamped with eagle (tax mark), "M" crowned (Mexico City) and "FCDA" (genuine marks of Antonio Forcada de La Plaza) and owner's mark, "ROZAS."

PLATTER (Fig. 22-A), Mexico, 1791–1818. Probably from shop of master silversmith José María Rodallega (1772–1812). Length: 35.9 cm; width: 23.8 cm; depth: 2.5 cm; weight: 751.28 gr. Stamped with eagle (tax mark), "M" crowned (Mexico City) and "FCDA" (genuine marks of Antonio Forcada de La Plaza) and "RDGA" (probably Rodallega's shop mark).

PLATTER (Fig. 22-B), Mexico, after 1895 (probably an early 20th c. reproduction of colonial piece). With beaded rim. Length: 45.7 cm; width: 29.2 cm; depth: 2.5 cm; weight: 1.304 kg. Stamped with "800."

PLATTER (Fig. 23-A), Guatemala, 18th c. With thumb print rim. Length: 31.2 cm; width: 22.8 cm; depth: 2 cm; weight: 793.8 gr. Stamped with lion over three peaks (stands for tax and quality).

ROUND PLATTER (not illustrated), Guatemala, 18th c. With six lobes. Faint "Luz Ramires de Wading (or Vlading) inscribed on bottom of rim. Diameter: 31.7 cm; depth: 2.8 cm; weight: 893.03 gr. Stamped with crown and Santiago over two peaks (both stand for tax and quality).

PLAIN ROUND PLATTER (not illustrated), Guatemala, 18th c. Letter "A" scratched on bottom. Diameter: 36.2 cm; depth: 3.5 cm; weight: 1.332 kg. Stamped with crown (stands for tax and quality), one undistinguishable mark and "EBAR" (may be contraction of silversmith's name "Escobar").

SIX-LOBED ROUND PLATTER (not illustrated), Mexico, 1791–1818. With script initials "G. E. F." and "T." scattered around top of rim. Diameter: 31.1 cm; depth: 2.5 cm; weight: 800.89 gr. Stamped with eagle (tax mark), "M" crowned (Mexico City), and name of silversmith José Careaga, examined in Mexico City in 1790.

ROUND SERVING TRAY WITH HANDLES (like Fig. 27-A), Mexico, 1733–1778. Diameter: 33 cm; depth: 3.2 cm; weight: 1.262 kg. Stamped with eagle and pillars of Hercules (one stands for tax and other for quality—which is which not certain), and "GOZA" over "LEZ" (genuine marks of Chief Assayer Diego González de la Cueva) and name of silversmith Gallo Espinosa de los Monteros, examined in Mexico City in 1763.

ONE BEADED PLATE (Fig. 24-B), Guatemala, 18th c. Diameter: 22.8 cm; depth: 1.9 cm; weight: 425.25 gr. Stamped with crown, Santiago over two peaks (both stand for tax and quality) and identified silversmith's mark "D. ANGULO."

FOUR PLAIN PLATES (Fig. 25-B), Mexico, 18th c. Alike except for size.

One inscribed with "Doña María Josepha Calderon y Bermejo" and a ranch brand in the shape of a "Y," one with inscriptions "Sirvo a casa Farnísa" and a scratchy "TR," and another stamped with owner's mark "BARRIO." Average diameter: 23.4 cm; average depth: 1.8 cm; average weight: 510.3 gr. Three stamped with eagle (tax mark), "M" crowned (Mexico City) and "GNZ" (genuine marks of Chief Assayer Diego González de la Cueva, 1733–1778). One with eagle (tax mark), "M" crowned (Mexico City) and "FCDA" (genuine marks of Chief Assayer Antonio Forcada y La Plaza, 1791–1818) and name of silversmith Francisco Galván, *veedor* in Mexico City in 1799.

TWELVE SIX-LOBED PLATES (Fig. 28-A), Mexico and Guatemala, 18th and 19th c. With cyma borders. Average diameter: 24 cm; average depth: 2 cm; average weight: 453.6 gr. Six with Mexican marks: two with eagle (tax mark), "M" crowned (Mexico City) and "GNZ" (genuine marks of Chief Assayer Diego González de la Cueva, 1733–1778), one with eagle (tax mark), "M" crowned (Mexico City) and "LNC" or "LIN" over "CE" (genuine marks of Chief Assayer José Antonio Lince González, 1779–1788), two with eagle (tax mark) "M" with "o" (Mexico City) and "BTON" (genuine marks of Chief Assayer Cayetano Buitrón, 1823–1843) and one with pillars of Hercules (tax and hallmark of quality). Three stamped with Guatemalan crowns and Santiagos over two peaks (all stand for tax and quality). Three either unmarked or with undistinguishable dies.

*ONE EIGHT-LOBED PLATE (Fig. 28-B), Mexico, 18th c. Alternating plain and ogee lobes with cyma border. Inscribed with amateurish "CE" on bottom. Diameter: 23.4 cm; depth: 2.5

cm; weight: 963.9 gr. Indistinguishable mark.

ONE DINNER PLATE (like Fig. 31-A), Mexico, 1791–1818. Plain edge with six lobes. With monogram "YMP" on bottom. Diameter: 24.1 cm; depth: 2 cm; weight: 453.6 gr. Stamped with eagle (tax mark), "M" crowned (Mexico City) and "FCDA" (genuine marks of Chief Assayer Antonio Forcada y La Plaza) name of master silversmith Alejandro Antonio de Cañas and owner's name "POSSE."

TWO SALAD PLATES (Fig. 27-B), Mexico, 18th c. With five plain edged lobes. Diameter: 16.5 cm; depth: 1.6 cm; weight (each): 262.24 gr. One stamped with eagle (tax mark), "M" crowned (Mexico City) and "FCDA" (genuine marks of Chief Assayer Antonio Forcada y La Plaza, 1791–1818). One unmarked.

*TWO SALAD PLATES (Fig. 29-B), Guatemala, 18th c. With false (stamped) beading. Alike except for size and marks. Average diameter: 17.3 cm; average depth: 1.3 cm; average weight: 248.06 gr. One stamped with crown and Santiago over two peaks, the other with crown and Capital "S" (Señor Santiago) on either side of one peak (all stand for tax and quality).

TWO SALAD PLATES (Fig. 29-A), Mexico, 1823–43. Seven lobes with cyma borders. Alike except for size. Average diameter: 15.5 cm; average depth: 2 cm; average weight: 198.45 gr. Both stamped with eagle (tax mark), "M" with "o" (Mexico City) and "BTON" (genuine marks of Chief Assayer Cayetano Buitrón).

ONE SALAD PLATE (Fig. 30-A), Guatemala, 18th c. Five lobes with cyma border. Script monogram "MR" on bottom. Diameter: 17.2 cm; depth: 1.5 cm; weight: 212.63 gr. Stamped with one crown (stands for tax and quality.

FOUR PLAIN SALAD PLATES (Fig. 30-B), Mexico, 1823–43. Plain edges. Average diameter: 21 cm; average depth: 1.5 cm; average weight: 396.9 gr. All stamped with eagle (tax mark), "M" with "o" (Mexico City) and "BTON" (genuine marks of Chief Assayer Cayetano Buitrón). One with name of Manuel Soriano, silversmith active in Mexico City in 1831, and the name of silver shop "SAUTO." One with name of master silversmith Alejandro Antonio de Cañas (1755–1830s) and owner's mark "SANTO" on top rim. Two with name of master silversmith José Miguel Mexía, examined in Mexico City in 1791.

THREE SALAD PLATES (like Fig. 31-A), Guatemala, 18th c. Six lobes with plain edges. Alike except for size. One with inscription "Mercedes Lopez Colon Y Aguirra," one with "Dn Josef Bent a del Trade" and one with "Maria de la luz Asturias y Wading (or Vlading)." Average diameter: 17.5 cm; average depth: 1.7 cm; average weight: 240.98 gr. All stamped with crowns and Santiago over two peaks (all stand for tax and quality).

ONE SAUCER (like Fig. 25-B), Mexico, 1791–1818. With plain edge. Diameter: 14.9 cm; depth: 1.2 cm; weight: 177.19 gr. Stamped with eagle (tax mark), "M" crowned (Mexico City) and "FCDA" (genuine marks of Antonio Forcada y La Plaza).

EIGHT SALT DISHES (not illustrated), Mexico, 19th c. Alike except for marks. Average diameter: 8.2 cm; average depth: 1 cm; average weight: 56.7 gr. Four stamped with eagle (tax mark, "M" with "o" (Mexico City) and "BTON" (genuine marks of Chief Assayer Cayetano Buitrón, 1823–1843), four with faint marks which may be forgeries.

FLUTED BOWL (Fig. 31-B), Guatemala, 18th c. Etched border above shallow flutes. Letters "LZ" scratched on bottom. Diameter: 15.8 cm; depth: 7.3 cm; weight: 503.21 gr. No marks.

*TWO-HANDLED BOWL (Fig. 33-A), probably Mexican, 18th c. Undecorated, with inverted base. "Doña Maria Antonio Rocha" inscribed on bottom. Diameter: 20.4 cm; height: 11.1 cm; weight: 730.01 gr. No marks.

*LOBED BOWL (Fig. 35-B), Mexico, late 18th or early 19th c. Monogram "Dn. TAV" on bottom. Diameter: 14.7 cm; depth: 6.3 cm; weight: 411.08 gr. Stamped with crown (Guatemalan), eagle (probably tax mark) and unidentified silversmith's mark "RAMIREZ." May have been stamped by Oaxaca *Caja Real*.

LOW BOWL (not illustrated), Guatemala, 18th c. Decorated with small floral spray on side. Diameter: 18.4 cm; height: 4.4 cm; weight: 318.94 gr. Stamped with crown and Santiago over two peaks (stand for tax and quality).

*LARGE BASIN (Fig. 35-A), Mexico, 1823–1843. Etched floral design and monogram "F.B." in bottom. Diameter: 38.1 cm; depth: 8.9 cm; weight: 1.7 kg. Stamped with eagle (tax mark), "M" with "o" (Mexico City) and "BTON" (genuine marks of Chief Assayer Cayetano Buitrón).

BRASERILLO (Fig. 32-B), probably Mexican, 19th c. With serpent feet. Script initials "GH" on bottom. Length (tray): 21 cm; width (tray): 13.6 cm; diameter (cup): 8.2 cm; height: 12 cm; weight: 368.55 gr. No marks.

TWO JIGGER CUPS (not illustrated), Mexico, after 1895. Diameter: 5.7 cm; height: 6.3 cm; weight (each): 155.93 gr. Both stamped with eagles and the number "881" (marks used after 1895

to indicate content of pure silver in thousandths).

PAIR OF CUPS (not illustrated), Mexico, 18th c. Engraved with script initials "T.M." Diameter (tops): 8.2 cm; diameter (bottoms): 5.7 cm; heights: 8.9 cm; weight (each): 198.45 gr. No marks.

CUP (Fig. 39-B), Mexico, 1823–1843. Diameter (top): 9.4 cm; height: 8.9 cm; weight: 219.71 gr. Stamped with eagle (tax mark), "M" with "o" (Mexico City) and "BTON" (genuine marks of Chief Assayer Cayetano Buitrón) and name of silversmith Antonio Goderes, documented as active in Mexico City in 1831.

*TEACUP (Fig. 40-B), Mexico, late 19th or early 20th c. Reproduction. Diameter (top): 10.1 cm; diameter (base): 5.3 cm; height: 7 cm; weight: 184.28 gr. Forged marks (probably of Buitrón's).

BEAKER (Fig. 46-B), Mexico, 17th c. With initials "M. R." scratched on bottom. Diameter (top): 10.2 cm; diameter (bottom): 7.6 cm; height: 12.1 cm; weight: 304.76 gr. Illegible mark.

*LADLE (Fig. 50-A), Mexico, 1791–1818. Length: 33 cm; diameter (bowl): 9.5 cm; weight: 283.5 gr. Stamped with eagle (tax mark), "M" crowned (Mexico City) and "FCDA" (genuine marks of Chief Assayer Antonio Forcada y La Plaza) and name of master silversmith Antonio Caamaño, *veedor* in Mexico City in 1800, 1801 and 1808.

LADLE (Fig. 50-B), Mexico, 18th c. With black wooden handle. Length: 33.2 cm; diameter (bowl): 11.1 cm; weight: 177.19 gr. No marks.

*TRAY FOR CANDLE SNUFFER (Fig. 53-A), Mexico, 1791–1818. Length: 24.1 cm; width: 10.2 cm; depth: 3.2 cm; weight: 382.73 gr. Stamped with eagle (tax mark), "M" crowned (Mexico City) and "FCDA" (genuine marks of Chief Assayer Antonio Forcada y La Plaza) and indistinguishable silversmith's mark.

*CANDLE SNUFFER (Fig. 53-B), Mexico, late 18th or early 19th c. Initials "TM" scratched on bottom. Length: 16.5 cm; width (handles): 6.3 cm; weight: 106.31 gr. No marks.

SILVER CARAFE (Fig. 78), Northern Provincial, Colonial period. Diameter (widest point): 10.2 cm; height: 21.5 cm; weight: 375.64 gr. No marks.

MATCHING TEASPOON AND FORK (Fig. 52-C), Mexico, 19th c. Perfectly plain. Length: 15.2 cm; weight (each): 28.35 gr. No marks.

SEVEN PLAIN TEASPOONS (Fig. 52-D), Mexico, 19th c. Four with initials "F. G.," two with heavily reinforced shoulders and "T.D.A.," one with "T.G.L." engraved on backs. Average length: 18 cm; average weight: 63.79 gr. No marks.

FIFTEEN DECORATED TABLE-SPOONS (Fig. 52-A), Guatemala, 18th c. Twelve matching with "L. D. T. D." engraved on backs. Average length: 18.8 cm; average weight: 63.79 gr. No marks.

SEVENTEEN DECORATED TEA-SPOONS (Fig. 52-A), Guatemala, early 19th c. Eleven matching. Nine with similar floral designs. Thirteen with "T. M. D. Durán" engraved on backs, one with "Maria del S Vasquez." Average length: 17 cm; average weight: 56.7 gr. No marks.

TEN DECORATED DINNER FORKS (Fig. 52-A), Guatemala, early 19th c. Six matching with "T. M. D. Durán" on backs. Average length: 17 cm; average weight: 49.61 gr. No marks.

CATALOGUE

INTERNATIONAL BUSINESS MACHINES COLLECTION

MUSEUM OF NEW MEXICO, SANTA FE

PAIR OF CANDLESTICKS (Fig. 7) Paraguay, c. 1700. One shorter than the other because of damage. Heights: 57.5 cm and 54 cm; diameter (bases): 20 cm; weights: 2.44 kg. and 2.39 kg. No marks.

CANDELABRUM WITH NIMBUS (Fig. 8), Paraguay, late 17th c. Jesuit mission style. Height: 56.5 cm; width (widest point): 42 cm; weight: 1.8 kg. No marks.

PAIR OF CANDLESCONCES (Fig. 9), Paraguay, late 17th c. Jesuit mission style. Height: 34.5 cm; width (wings): 21.5 cm; weight: 467.78 gr. No marks.

BAPTISMAL SHELL (Fig. 11), Peru, late 18th c. Width: 42.5 cm; depth: 33 cm; height: 8.5; weight: 1.5 kg. No marks.

CANDELABRUM (Fig. 17), Peru, mid-19th c. Style of Peruvian independence. Height: 50 cm; diameter (base): 14.5 cm; width (widest point): 43 cm; weight: 2 kg. No marks.

SERVING TRAY (Fig. 24-A), Argentina, 18th or 19th c. With *chispa* design. Diameter: 38.5 cm; depth: 2 cm; weight: 949.73 gr. Stamped with unidentified silversmith's or assayer's mark "LANAO" and the number "900" (meaning unknown).

PLATTER (not illustrated), Argentina, 18th or 19th c. With *chispa* design arranged like fleur-de-lys. Length: 51.4 cm; width: 35.5 cm; depth: 2.6 cm; weight: 1.26 kg. Stamped with silversmith's or assayer's mark "LANAO" and number "900" (meaning unknown).

LARGE PLATE OR SHALLOW BOWL (Fig. 62-A), *Norteño*, Colonial period. Script initials "L. C." scratched under rim with small burin. Diameter: 33 cm; depth: 4.2 cm; weight: 1.12 kg. No marks.

SAHUMADOR (Fig. 41), Chile, mid-19th c. Turkey sitting on a twig. Diameter (base): 12.5 cm; height: 16 cm; weight: 326.03 gr. No marks.

SILVER OLLA (Fig. 67-A), *Norteño*, Colonial period. With script initial "L" engraved on one wedding ring handle and "T" on the other. Diameter (widest point): 15 cm; height: 15 cm; weight: 637.88 gr. No marks.

GRAVY OR SAUCE BOAT (Fig. 65-B), *Norteño*, Colonial period. Length (overall): 31 cm; width (widest point): 12.5 cm; height (overall): 14.3 cm; weight: 963.9 gr. No marks.

FLARED PITCHER OR SAUCE DISH (Fig. 64-B), *Norteño*, Colonial period. With script letters "M. F." on bottom. Diameter (top): 12 cm; diameter (bottom): 6 cm; height: 13 cm; weight: 389.81 gr. No marks.

MATE CUP (Fig. 46-A), Peru, late 18th or early 19th c. Andean style. Carved gourd mounted in silver. Birds on rim. Diameter: 8.5 cm; height: 13 cm; weight: 184.28 gr. No marks.

MATE CUP (Fig. 46-B), Bolivia, late 18th c. With bird handles. Diameter (saucer): 12.5 cm; height (overall): 11.5 cm; weight: 233.89 gr. No marks.

BOMBILLA (Fig. 47-B), Peru, early 19th c. Sipping tube. Length 21.5 cm; weight: 49.61 gr. No marks.

CATALOGUE

LYMAN COLLECTION

MUSEUM OF NEW MEXICO, SANTA FE

FILIGREE TRAY (Fig. 21-A), Peru, 18th c. Ayacucho "silver lace." Length: 32 cm; width: 25 cm; weight: 574.09 gr. No marks.

LARGE PLATTER OR TRAY (Fig. 61-B), *Norteño*, Colonial period. Length: 62 cm; width: 46 cm; depth: 2 cm; weight: 2.35 kg. No marks.

FISH PLATTER (Fig. 23-B), Colombia, 19th c. Length: 56.4 cm; width: 29.5 cm; depth: 4.5 cm; weight: 1.01 kg. Unidentified mark.

PLATTER OR SHALLOW DISH (not illustrated), rural Colombia, Colonial period. With ten lobes. Length: 46.5 cm; width: 33.6 cm; depth: 4.3 cm. weight: 1.01 kg. No marks.

SHALLOW DISH (Fig. 64-A), rural Colombia, Colonial period. With eight lobes. Length: 37 cm; width: 25 cm; depth: 4.5 cm; weight: 687.49 gr. No marks.

CANDY BOWL (not illustrated), Colombia. Probably modern. Completely covered with repoussé and stamped decorations. Diameter (bowl): 15 cm; height (overall): 18 cm; weight: 595.35 gr. No marks.

PLATTER OR SHALLOW BOWL (Fig. 63-B), rural Colombia. Colonial period. With six flattened lobes. Length: 30.5 cm; width: 23 cm; depth: 3.9 cm; weight: 453.6 gr. No marks.

SCALLOPED PLATE (Fig. 26-B), Colombia, 18th or 19th c. Diameter: 25 cm; depth: 2 cm; weight: 481.95 gr. No marks.

MATE CUP (Fig. 48-B), Peru, late 18th or early 19th c. Andean style. Carved gourd mounted in silver with figure of hunter on handle. Diameter (widest point): 7.5 cm; height (overall): 14 cm; weight: 127.58 gr. No marks.

CUP (Fig. 69-A), rural Colombia, late 19th c. Diameter (top): 8 cm; diameter (bottom): 5.5 cm; height: 5.1 cm; weight: 77.96 gr. Patches of solder may have been an attempt to simulate legal marks.

TWO-HANDLED CUP (Fig. 40-A), Mexico, late 19th or early 20th c. Tulip shaped. Diameter (top): 6.2 cm; diameter (base): 4.5 cm; height: 7 cm; weight: 120.49 gr. No marks.

TWO-HANDLED CUP (not illustrated), Mexico, late 19th or early 20th c. With flared sides and cast handles similar to those on cup in Fig. 35-A. Amateurish monogram composed of the letters "J VEZ" with an "N" above and "R" with an "A" above scratched on bottom. Diameter (bottom): 6 cm; height: 6.2 cm; weight: 120.49 gr. No marks.

TEACUP (Fig. 39-A), Mexico, after 1895. Footed, with tiny cast handle similar in design to those on cup in Fig. 35-A. Diameter (top): 7.4 cm; diameter (base): 3.8 cm; height: 7 cm; weight: 77.96 gr. Stamped with number "30" on one side of rim and "L 900" opposite (signifies standard and content of silver in thousandths).

CUP (not illustrated), Northern Provincial, Colonial period. Straight sides with triangular design scratched on border around top. Diameter (top): 6.4 cm; diameter (bottom): 5.7 cm; height 6 cm; weight: 106.31 gr. No marks.

TEACUP (not illustrated), Mexico, late 19th or early 20th c. With inscription "L de C" engraved on side. Diameter (top): 7.2 cm; diameter (base): 4.2 cm; height: 6 cm; weight: 106.31 gr. No marks.

CATALOGUE

FIELD COLLECTION

UNIVERSITY ART MUSEUM, ALBUQUERQUE

HELMET-SHAPED EWER (Fig. 15), Mexico, 1861–62 or 1867–68. Height: 27 cm; diameter (widest point): 21.9 cm; diameter (base): 12.1 cm; weight: 1.31 kg. Stamped with eagle (tax mark), "M" with "o" (Mexico City) and "CASTILLO" (genuine marks of Chief Assayer Antonio del Castillo).

FOOTED SALVER (Fig. 26-A), Mexico, 18th or 19th c. Diameter: 33.3 cm; depth: 3.2 cm; weight: 992.25 gr. Forged mark (eagle) probably stamped in early 20th c. to make it more attractive to antique collectors.

PLATTER OR LARGE BOWL (Fig. 63-A), Northern Provincial, Colonial period. Length: 39.8 cm; width: 28 cm; depth: 9.2 cm; weight: 1.3 kg. No marks.

CRUET TRAY (Fig. 57-B), Northern Provincial, Colonial period. Length: 21 cm; width: 10.2 cm; weight: 368.55 gr. No marks.

TWO SERVING TRAYS (like Fig. 27-A), Mexico, 18th c. Alike except for size. Larger tray, diameter: 35.7 cm; depth: 3 cm; weight: 1.16 kg. Stamped with pillars of Hercules (tax and hallmark of quality), unidentified mark "LXZR" and monogram "oN." Smaller tray, diameter 33.2 cm; depth: 3.5 cm; weight: 1.25 kg. Stamped with eagle and pillars of Hercules (tax mark and hallmark of quality—which is which, not certain) and "G N Z" (genuine marks of Chief Assayer Diego González de la Cueva, 1733–1778), unidentified "Z" with "o" on diagonal and monogram "XR."

SMALL TRAY (Fig. 14-A), Mexico, 1837. Probably an alms dish. Length: 19.1 cm; width: 12.5 cm; weight: 255.15 gr. Inscribed with *"ESTE PLATO LO MANDO HACER EL S.C.D.M.C. LEMUS EL MES D MAYO D 1837"* which translated reads "This plate ordered made for the Señor Cura Don M. C. Lemus the month of May 1837," followed by indistinct ecclesiastical stamp.

LARGE BOWL (Fig. 65-A), Northern Provincial, Colonial period. Diameter: 43.6 cm; depth: 14.3 cm; weight: 2.3 kg. No marks.

SMALL BOWL (Fig. 67-B), Northern Provincial, Colonial period. Diameter (rim): 12.7 cm; height: 5.7 cm; weight: 368.55 gr. No marks.

LARGE FLUTED BOWL (Fig. 32-A), Mexico, 1791–1818. By master silversmith Antonio Caamaño who served as *Veedor* in Mexico City in 1799 and 1801. Diameter: 34.7 cm; depth: 8.6 cm; weight: 1.29 kg. Stamped with eagle (tax mark), "M" crowned (Mexico City) and "FCDA" (genuine marks of Chief Assayer Antonio Forcada y La Plaza 1791–1818) and Caamaño's name.

BRASERILLO (Fig. 36-A), Mexico, 19th c. Length (tray): 21 cm; width (tray): 12.7 cm; length (bowl): 12.1 cm; width (bowl): 9.5 cm; height: 7.6 cm; weight: 368.55 gr. No marks.

INCENSE BOAT (Fig. 59-A), Northern Provincial, Colonial period. Initials "R. N." scratched on rim. Height (with hinges): 8.9 cm; length (with handles): 12.7 cm; width (bowl): 9.5 cm; weight: 283.5 gr. No marks.

BRASERILLO (not illustrated), Mexico,

18th or 19th c. Name "Ro Zepeda" inscribed on bottom. Diameter (bowl): 11.1 cm; diameter (plate): 16.2 cm; height: 8.5 cm; weight: 396.9 gr. No marks.

STRAIGHT-SIDED BOWL (Fig. 68-B), Northern Provincial, Colonial period. Has bolt through middle of bottom, suggesting that it was originally a *braserillo*. Diameter: 12.7 cm; height: 5.4 cm; weight: 368.55 gr. Incised with scratchy "A" and triangle. No marks.

FLUTED BOWL (Fig. 66-A), Northern Provincial, Colonial period. Diameter: 14 cm; depth: 6.4 cm; weight: 340.2 gr. No marks.

BUTTER PLATE (Not illustrated), Mexico, after 1895. Could be a salt dish. Diameter: 8.9 cm; depth: .6 cm; weight: 85.05 gr. Stamped with eagle and "900" (indicating content of silver in thousandths). Used by Mexican mints after 1895. Sometimes "L" (for legal standard) used instead of eagle.

TEN PLAIN PLATES (like Fig. 30-B), Mexico, 19th c. Average diameter: 21.5 cm; average depth: 1.9 cm; average weight: 453.6 gr. Two stamped with rampant lion (tax mark), "M" crowned (Mexico City) and "DVLA" (possibly genuine marks of Chief Assayer Joáquin Dávila Madrid 1819–1823), one of which also has name of master silversmith José Felipe Mexía, licensed in 1815, and owner's mark "D. SAENZ." Eight without hallmarks, stamped with owner's mark "J. Marquez."

FIVE-LOBED PLATE (like Fig. 30-A), Mexico, 1791–1818. With cyma border. Diameter: 23.2 cm; depth: 2.4 cm; weight: 538.65 gr. Monogram "TPN" hand scratched on bottom. Stamped with eagle (tax mark), "M" crowned (Mexico City) and "FCDA" (genuine marks of Chief Assayer Antonio Forcada y La Plaza) and

"RDGA" which may be shop-mark of master silversmith José María Rodallega (1772–1812).

SIX-LOBED PLATE (like Fig. 28-A), Guatemala, 18th c. With cyma border. Diameter: 22.3 cm; depth: 1.9 cm; weight: 453.6 gr. Crude monogram "R. A." on bottom. Stamped with crown, Santiago over two peaks (both stand for tax and quality) and an incomplete silversmith's mark "MAR--F" over "ARES" (unidentified).

EIGHT-LOBED PLATE (like Fig. 28-B), Mexico, 1733–1788. Alternating plain and ogee lobes with cyma border. Diameter: 23.5 cm; depth: 2.5 cm; weight: 453.6 gr. Stamped with eagle and pillars of Hercules (tax mark and hallmark of quality—which is which, not certain) and "GNZ" (genuine, but worn, marks of Chief Assayer Diego González de la Cueva) and a deliberately defaced silversmith's mark. Inscribed with a crude "A" "XX" and amateurish "teresa Garacia" (probably misspelled).

PLATE OR SHALLOW BOWL (Fig. 62-B), Northern Provincial, Colonial period. Six lobes with flat tooled border. Diameter: 22.3 cm; depth: 4.1 cm; weight: 396.9 gr. Inscribed with "R. C. 2" and name "Ty . . . . ." executed in series of dots on bottom. No marks.

SIX SIX-LOBED PLATES (Fig. 31-A), Mexico, late 18th or early 19th c. With plain edges. Average diameter: 24.2 cm; average depth: 1.9 cm; average weight: 524.48 gr. Three with eagle (tax mark), "M" crowned (Mexico City) with "FCDA" (genuine marks of Chief Assayer Antonio Forcada y La Plaza, 1791–1818) and name of master silversmith Alejandro Antonio de Cañas. Two (genuinely old) stamped with eagle, crown and "FOR" over "CADA" (probably forged Forcada marks) and name of silversmith Francisco Galván, licensed in Mexico City, 1799 and 1807. All five stamped with owner's mark "CHABES." One, which may be much older, stamped with owner's mark B. MENDA-ROSQUETA" and "ZALDIVAR" followed by a small die with a crown over "D".

FIVE FIVE-LOBED PLATES (like Fig. 27-B), Mexico, 18th or 19th c. With plain edges. Average diameter: 23.7 cm; average depth: 2.4 cm; average weight: 510.3 gr. All stamped (probably later) with almost illegible forged Mexican marks (two may be forgeries of Forcada's). One stamped with owner's marks "CHABES" and "CARTAM."

CUP (not illustrated), probably Mexican, late 19th c. Diameter (top): 10.2 cm; diameter (foot): 4.5 cm; height: 8.6 cm; weight: 212.63 gr. No marks.

CUP (not illustrated), Mexico, 19th c. Diameter (top): 11.6 cm; diameter (base): 5.2 cm; weight: 198.45 gr. Stamped with two illegible marks and "MHRRAZ" (probably a forgery of Chief Assayer Mucharriz' marks, 1868–1880).

CUP (not illustrated), United States, late 19th c. Diameter (top): 8.9 cm; diameter (base): 5 cm; height: 6.4 cm; weight: 170.1 gr. Stamped with "H. H. HOLMAN & CO. PURE COIN."

CUP (not illustrated), probably Mexican, probably 19th c. Diameter (top): 11.8 cm; diameter (base): 5 cm; height: 5.7 cm; weight: 425.25 gr. Amateurish monograms "M," "S" and "JMB." No marks.

MUG WITH SERPENT HANDLE (Fig. 42), Mexico, dated 1866. Diameter (top): 9.2 cm; diameter (bottom): 7.3 cm; height: 10.5 cm; weight: 411.08 gr. Probably an old beaker to which 19th c. handle has

been attached. Handle inscribed on one side with "C. G. A." and Jo 20 año de 1866" on the other. No marks.

MUG (Fig. 74), Northern Provincial, Colonial period. Diameter (top): 9.7 cm; diameter (bottom): 6.4 cm; height: 10.5 cm; weight: 368.55 gr. No marks.

PAIR OF MUGS (not illustrated), Mexico, 18th c. Diameter (tops): 10.2 cm; diameter (bottoms): 10 cm; heights: 11.5 cm; weight (each): 368.55 gr. Perhaps old beakers to which 18th c. handles have been attached. No marks.

PAIR OF MUGS (Fig. 45-A), Mexico, probably early 18th c. Diameter (tops): 9.2 cm; diameter (bottoms): 7 cm; heights: 9.9 cm; weight (each): 297.68 gr. No marks.

MUG (not illustrated), probably Mexican, probably 18th c. Diameter (top): 8.6 cm; diameter (bottom): 6.7 cm; height: 10.2 cm; weight: 311.85 gr. Perhaps old beaker to which 18th c. handle has been attached. No marks.

MUG (not illustrated), Mexico, late 19th c. Diameter (top): 10.2 cm; diameter (bottom): 6.4 cm; height: 12.1 cm; weight: 396.9 gr. With forged Mexican marks. Inscribed with a brand and a monogram "Ro." Stamped with "ARDA." No marks.

MUG (similar to Fig. 45-A), Mexico, 18th c. Diameter (top): 9.9 cm; diameter (bottom): 7.3 cm; height: 10.8 cm; weight: 368.55 gr. Inscribed with crude "F" and "G" on bottom and faint "Trinidad C. de Baca" on side. No marks.

MUG (Fig. 73), Northern Provincial, Colonial period. Diameter (top): 7.6 cm; diameter (bottom): 7 cm; height: 10.8 cm; weight: 396.9 gr. Shaped reinforcing plate bolted to inside at top of handle. Inscribed with "Pino" on bottom. No marks.

MUG (Fig. 71), Northern Provincial, Colonial period. Diameter (top): 7 cm; diameter (bottom): 5 cm; height: 10.5

cm; weight: 255.15 gr. No marks.

MUG (not illustrated), Mexico, probably 18th c. Diameter (top): 8.9 cm; diameter (bottom): 7.3 cm; height: 10.2 cm; weight: 283.5 gr. No marks.

MUG (not illustrated), Mexico, 19th c. Diameter (top): 9.2 cm; diameter (bottom): 5.4 cm; height: 11.5 cm; weight: 368.55 gr. Stamped with initials "M.I." No marks.

MUG (Fig. 75), Northern Provincial, Colonial period. Diameter (top): 9.2 cm; diameter (bottom): 7 cm; height: 11.4 cm; weight: 368.55 gr. Inscribed with "R. N." No marks.

MUG (Fig. 44), Mexico, late 18th or early 19th c. Diameter (top): 9.2 cm; diameter (bottom): 5.7 cm; height: 10.5 cm; weight: 396.9 gr. No marks.

MUG (Fig. 43), Mexico, 17th c. Diameter (top): 10.2 cm; diameter (bottom): 8.8 cm; height: 12.9 cm; weight: 765.45 gr. May be tankard described in de Vargas will of 1704. No marks.

TUMBLER (not illustrated). Austria, 19th c. Diameter (top): 7.6 cm; diameter (bottom): 6.7 cm; height: 8.1 cm; weight: 141.75 gr. Inset with five coins: four one-half talers of Frederick the Great of Prussia, dated 1750 and one (in bottom) two-mark piece of Charles XII of Sweden, dated 1701. Inscribed with initials "A. R." No marks.

STEMMED GOBLET (Fig. 77), Northern Provincial, Colonial period. Diameter (top): 7.3 cm; diameter (base): 5 cm; height: 13.5 cm; weight: 311.85 gr. Probably used for spoon holder. No marks.

SERVING FORK AND SPOON (Fig. 49), Mexico, 18th c. Length (fork): 33.4 cm; weight (fork): 191.36 gr.; length (spoon): 30.9 cm; weight (spoon): 141.75 gr. Spoon inscribed with "P.D.C." No marks.

NINE FORKS (not illustrated), Mexico, 19th c. Average length: 19.4 cm; average weight: 99.23 gr. Six stamped with eagle (tax mark), "M" with "o" (Mexico City) and "BTON" (Buitrón's mark, 1823–43). Six with name of master silversmith José María Martínez. May be forged. Three without marks.

ONE FORK (not illustrated), probably 17th c. Length: 19.2 cm; weight: 106.31 gr. With three prongs and flat handle. No marks.

TEN SPOONS (not illustrated), Mexico, 19th c. Average length: 18.8 cm; average weight: 99.23 gr. Five stamped with eagle (tax mark), "M" with "o" (Mexico City) and "BTON" (Buitrón's mark, 1823–1843), three of which are stamped with two silversmith's marks "M. PORTU" (for Manuel Portugués) and "CANAS" (Alejandro Antonio de Cañas). May be forged. Five without marks.

PAIR FLUTED CANDLESTICKS (not illustrated), Mexico, 19th c. Heights: 19.4 cm; widths (base): 8.5 cm; weight (each): 623.7 gr. One damaged. Stamped with two eagles and "BTON" (doubtful marks of Chief Assayer Cayetano Buitrón, 1823–43) and owner's mark "CHABES."

PAIR FLUTED CANDLESTICKS (not illustrated), 18th or 19th c. Heights: 13.7 cm; widths (base): 6.9 cm; weight (each): 425.25 gr. Like above except for size. Stamped with two eagles and "FOR" over "CADA" (forged marks of Chief Assayer Antonio Forcada y La Plaza 1791–1818) and three indistinguishable owner's marks.

TWO PEAR/SHAPED CANDLESTICKS (not illustrated), Mexico, probably 18th c. Diameters (base): 14 cm; heights: 33 cm; weight (each): 680.4 gr. Unusual because made in one piece. No marks.

ONE BALUSTER CANDLESTICK (not illustrated), probably Austrian, probably 19th c. Diameter (base): 12.5 cm; height: 25.5 cm; weight: 737.1 gr. Stamped with four unidentified marks which seem to be Germanic.

TABAQUERA (Fig. 79-B), Northern Provincial, dated 1887. Height: 7.6 cm; width: 5 cm; weight: 170.1 gr. Inscribed with "Nov. 15th, 1886 M. Montoya." No marks.

TABAQUERA (Fig. 79-C), Northern Provincial, Colonial period. Height: 5.7 cm; width: 3.8 cm; weight: 85.05 gr. Inscribed with initials "V.B." No marks.

APPENDIX II

Reproduced from Anderson's *The Art of the Silversmith in Mexico 1519–1936*, Vol. I, pp. 288–352.

22. SUMMARY OF GENUINE MARKS STAMPED ON MEXICAN SILVER

1524–1936

NO. PERIOD	MARK USED FOR STANDARD (OF QUALITY) AND OF THE TAX (20%)	REMARKS *Enlarged*
1524–1578	 	It is possible, but not certain, that this mark is the one used prior to 1578. The mark is enlarged, its actual size being the following: 
2 1579–1637	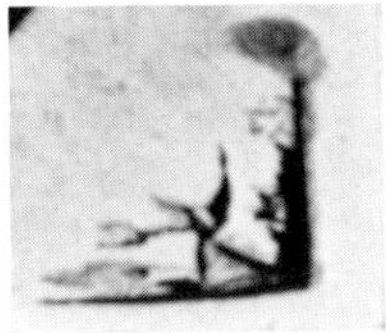	Although worn, which makes its reproduction difficult, the following mark is: the columns of Hercules crowned (adapted from the Spanish Arms), with an *M* between, which means "Mexico."
3 1638–1732		This mark is similar to the preceding one but smaller.

Figure 81

GENUINE AND FORGED MARKS OF THE PERIOD OF CHIEF ASSAYER DIEGO GONZÁLEZ DE LA CUEVA

1733–1778

NO.	DESCRIPTION	MARK OF THE CHIEF ASSAYER	HALL-MARK (QUALITY)	TAX MARK	REMARKS *Enlarged*
4	Genuine				
5	Genuine				
6	Genuine				

Figure 82

GENUINE AND FORGED MARKS OF THE PERIOD OF CHIEF ASSAYER DIEGO GONZÁLEZ DE LA CUEVA

1733–1778

NO. DESCRIPTION	MARK OF THE CHIEF ASSAYER	HALL-MARK (QUALITY)	TAX MARK	REMARKS *Enlarged*
6-A Forgery	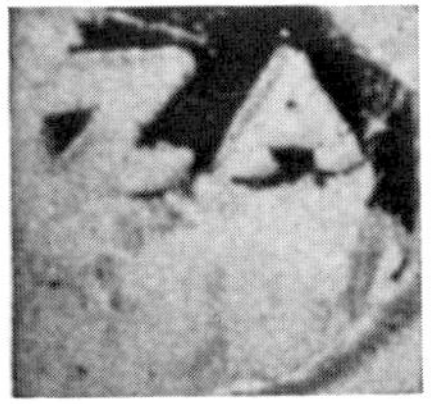	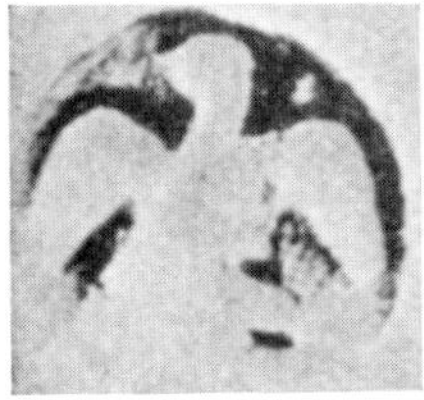	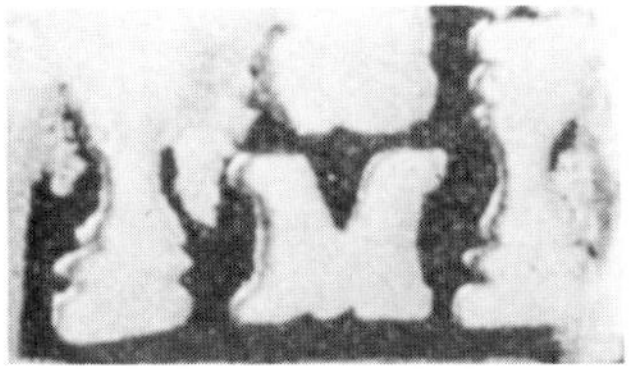	Forgery
6-B Forgery		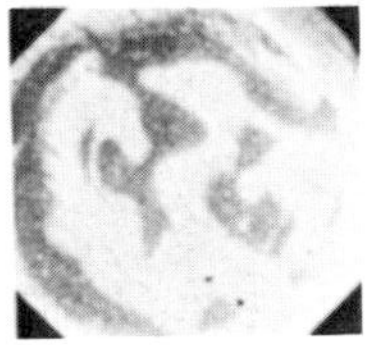	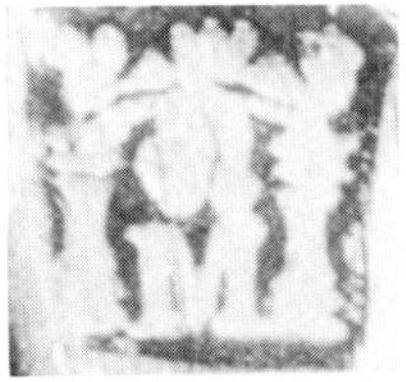	Forgery
6-C Forgery		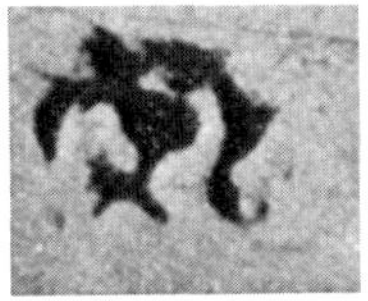		Forgery

Figure 83

182

GENUINE AND FORGED MARKS OF THE PERIOD OF CHIEF ASSAYER DIEGO GONZÁLEZ DE LA CUEVA

1733–1778

NO. DESCRIPTION	MARK OF THE CHIEF ASSAYER	HALL-MARK (QUALITY)	TAX MARK	REMARKS *Enlarged*
6-D Forgery				Forgery
6-E Forgery				Forgery From punches of Apolonio Guevara

Figure 84

GENUINE AND FORGED MARKS OF THE PERIOD OF CHIEF ASSAYER LIC. JOSÉ ANTONIO LINCE GONZÁLEZ

1779–1788

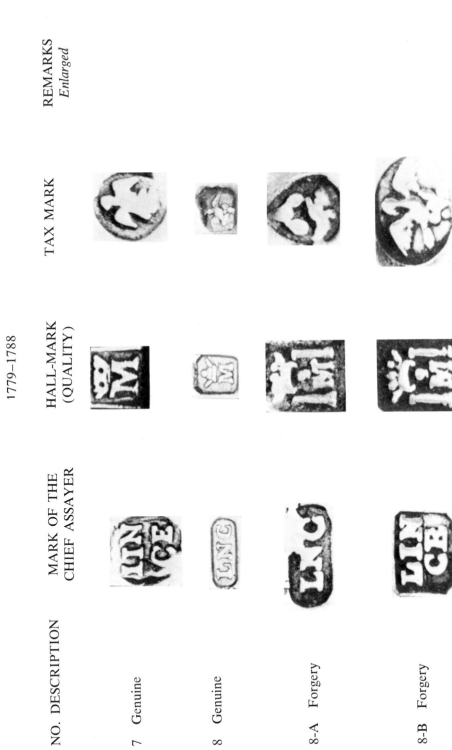

NO.	DESCRIPTION	MARK OF THE CHIEF ASSAYER	HALL-MARK (QUALITY)	TAX MARK	REMARKS *Enlarged*
7	Genuine				
8	Genuine				
8-A	Forgery				
8-B	Forgery				

Figure 85

GENUINE AND FORGED MARKS OF THE PERIOD OF CHIEF ASSAYER LIC. JOSÉ ANTONIO LINCE GONZÁLEZ

1779–88

DESCRIPTION	MARK OF THE CHIEF ASSAYER	HALL-MARK (QUALITY)	TAX MARK	REMARKS *Enlarged*
		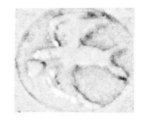		
Forgery				
Forgery				

Figure 86

GENUINE AND FORGED MARKS OF THE PERIOD OF CHIEF ASSAYER LIC. JOSÉ ANTONIO LINCE GONZÁLEZ

1779–1788

NO. DESCRIPTION	MARK OF THE CHIEF ASSAYER	HALL-MARK (QUALITY)	TAX MARK	REMARKS *Enlarged*
				From punches of Apolonio Guevara

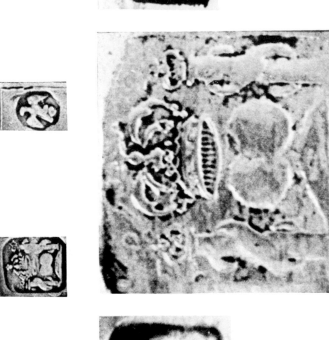

8-E Forgery

8-F Forgery

Figure 87

186

FORGERIES OF THE MARKS OF THE CHIEF ASSAYER FRANCISCO ARANCE Y COBOS
1789–90

Mark of the Chief Assayer

Tax-mark

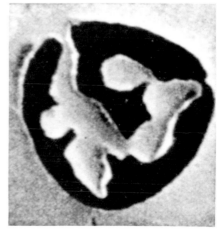

Hall-mark

Figure 88

GENUINE AND FORGED MARKS OF THE PERIOD OF CHIEF ASSAYER ANTONIO FORCADA Y LA PLAZA
1791–1818

NO.	DESCRIPTION	MARK OF THE CHIEF ASSAYER	HALL-MARK (QUALITY)	TAX MARK	REMARKS *Enlarged*
10	Genuine			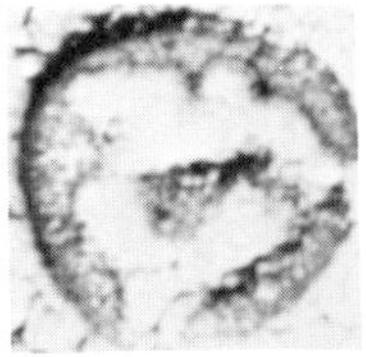	Another type of crown used with the same marks: 
11	Genuine				Quite common
12	Genuine	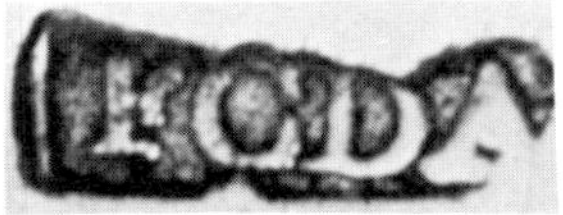		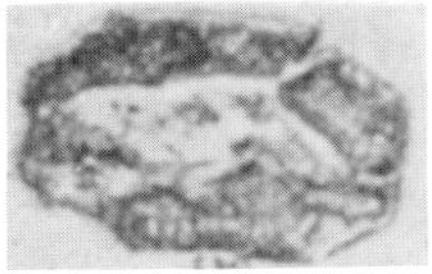	Rare
13	Genuine		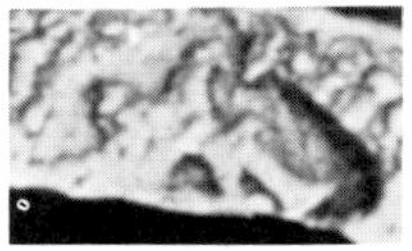		Rare

Figure 89

188

GENUINE AND FORGED MARKS OF THE PERIOD OF CHIEF ASSAYER ANTONIO FORCADA Y LA PLAZA
1791–1818

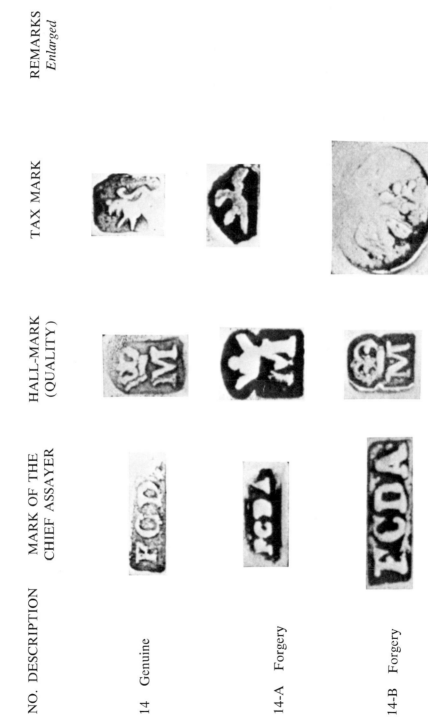

NO. DESCRIPTION	MARK OF THE CHIEF ASSAYER	HALL-MARK (QUALITY)	TAX MARK	REMARKS *Enlarged*
14 Genuine				
14-A Forgery				
14-B Forgery				

Figure 90

189

FORGERIES OF MADRID'S MARKS
1819–1823

MARK OF THE
CHIEF ASSAYER

HALL-MARK
(QUALITY)

TAX MARK

REMARKS

Forgeries

Forgeries

Figure 91

GENUINE AND FORGED MARKS OF THE PERIOD OF CHIEF ASSAYER CAYETANO BUITRÓN

1823–43

NO. DESCRIPTION	MARK OF THE CHIEF ASSAYER	HALL-MARK (QUALITY)	TAX MARK	REMARKS *Enlarged*
16 Genuine				These are the only genuine marks of the period of Buitrón that I have found. This is, by far, the most common of all authentic marks found on Mexican plate.
16-A Forgery			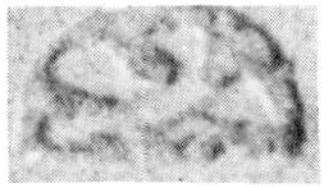	Forgery. Frequently found.
16-B Forgery			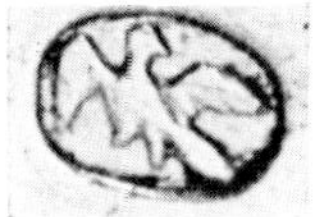	The *M* with the small *o* above is an excellent forgery.
16-C Forgery				Poor forgery. Quite common.
16-D Forgery			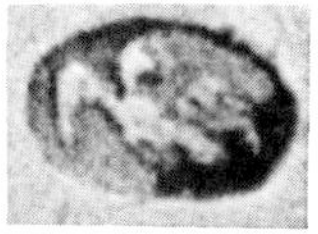	Rare

Figure 92

GENUINE AND FORGED MARKS OF THE PERIOD OF CHIEF ASSAYER CAYETANO BUITRÓN

1823–1843

NO. DESCRIPTION	MARK OF THE CHIEF ASSAYER	HALL-MARK (QUALITY)	TAX MARK	REMARKS *Enlarged*
				With these same punches of 'Bton' and the 'Eagle' the following was also used:
				Rare
				Very rare
16-E Forgery				
16-F Forgery				Forgery found in abundance.
16-G Forgery				
16-H Forgery				The forgery of the *M* crowned is remarkably well made.

Figure 93

SUMMARY OF THE GENUINE MARKS STAMPED ON MEXICAN PLATE
1524–1936

PERIOD	NO.	MARK OF THE CHIEF ASSAYER	HALL-MARK (QUALITY)	TAX MARK	REMARKS *Enlarged*
Of Chief Assayer Camacho 1856–1860 1863–1867	17			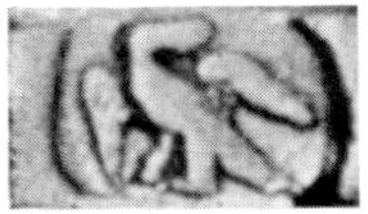	Camacho. No forgeries are found.
Of Chief Assayer Castillo 1861–1862 1867–1868	18			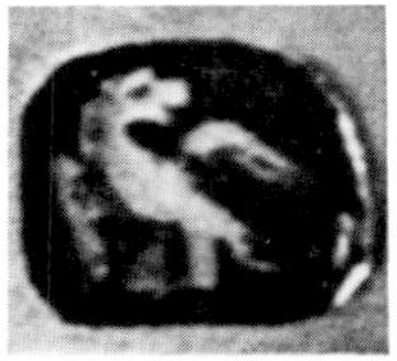	Castillo. No forgeries are found.
Of Chief Assayer Mucharraz 1868–1880	19			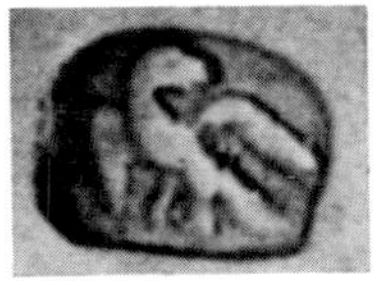	Mucharraz. No forgeries are found. The 'Eagle' used by Morales is from Buitrón's punch, which is still in use in the Mint in Mexico.
Of Chief Assayer Morales 1881–1889	20				
Of Chief Assayer Sáyago 1890–1893	21			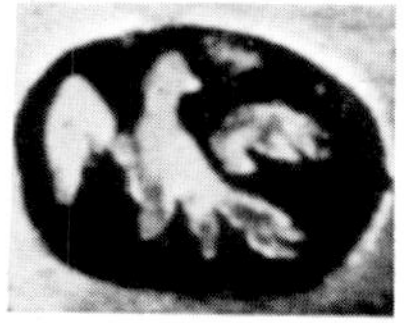	I have not found Sáyago's mark. Chief Assayer Obregón told me that Sáyago used Morales' punches the *M* with a small *o* above it and the 'Eagle.'

Figure 94

193

SUMMARY OF THE GENUINE MARKS STAMPED ON MEXICAN PLATE

1524–1936

PERIOD	NO.	MARK OF THE CHIEF ASSAYER	HALL-MARK (QUALITY)	TAX MARK	REMARKS *Enlarged*
1894–1895 Of Chief Assayer Obregón	22				
1895–1936	23	Not Used			On the Hall-mark the *L* means 'Ley' (standard) and the number *860* indicates the pure silver content in thousandths of the piece assayed. The Eagle is from the same punch used by Chief Assayers Buitrón, Morales, Sáyago and Obregón.

Figure 95

194

Marks from Punches in possessions of
the Silver Shop 'Maciel'
Actual Size

Enlarged marks from punches used by
Carillo y Mendoza as decorations

Marks from Apolonio
Guevara's forged punches
Actual size

A.

Actual Size   Enlarged

Actual Size

Enlarged

B. Hall-marks   San Luis Potosí

Figure 96

195

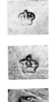

A. Typical examples of the individual owners' marks

B. The "R" Crowned

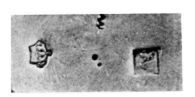

C. Hall-marks   Guatamala-Chiapas

Figure 97

APPENDIX III

SIGNIFICANT DOCUMENTS

I. List of all items accepted by the University of New Mexico from the executors of the Mary Lester Field estate, as tabulated in the Field will:

21 Volumes, limited edition, of William Shakespeare; 1 Robert Burns portfolio; Copper sugar shaker; Brass pestle & mortar; 1 Baumann wood block (gift of Mrs. Robert E. Dietz); 1 Copper pitcher; 1 Copper and brass pitcher; 2 Nichos (santos enclosed in tinware); 2 Candelabras; 1 Mahogany table; 1 Lamp—Mayan base; 4 Fiddle back chairs; 1 Opium bowl; 11 Old copper pestles; 1 Copper kettle with stand.

Collection of Spanish-Colonial silver, as follows; 9 forks; 8 spoons; 1 small spoon; 25 plates; 1 large deep platter—riveted handles; 1 large fluted bowl; 1 chalice; 2 small trays; 7 candlesticks; 1 brazier; 2 round service platters—handles; 1 large service fork; 1 large service spoon; 16 beakers; 4 tea (or coffee) cups; 1 bouillon cup; 2 snuff holders; 2 service bowls; 1 small covered dish—hinged covers; 1 oval dish and tray; 1 cup, coin insets; 1 scalloped tray with legs; 1 pitcher; 1 large bowl (wash bowl); 1 butter plate.

1 large display sideboard for containing silver.

Collection of Santos (Spanish and Mexican) as follows: 1 Virgin Pura (surrounded by angels); 1 Trinity; 1 San Miguel; 1 St. with child; 1 Sonora Remedions; 1 St. Anthony (baby missing); 1 St. Anthony (with baby); 2 Guadalupes; 1 Rosewood Madonna; 1 Madre Dolorosa; 3 others; San Acacio; 4 crosses.

5 Chimayos.

1 framed "marriage scarf."

II. Complete text of that part of the de Vargas will which refers to the silver discussed in this study as copied from a translation in Twitchell's *Spanish Archives of New Mexico,* Vol. I, p. 303.

In the same manner my attorney and executor, the same being my Lieutenant-General, Don Juan Paez Hurtado, will remit or sell at the best obtainable prices the following silverware:

1st.: Thirty small silver dishes, the fifth part taken, and twenty-four sealed with my coat-of-arms and weighing more than two marks.

Two large dishes which weigh twelve marks and ounces.

Six candle-sticks, with my coat-of-arms, and two pairs of candle snuffers, which weigh forty-two marks, more or less.

Twelve silver porringers which weigh twelve ounces, sealed with my coat-of-arms, the one-fifth taken.

One silver bowl, gilded with a siren, weighing sixteen and seventeen marks, more or less.

One small silver keg, with stopper and chain, the one-fifth part taken, weighing six marks.

One large plain tankard, weighing two marks and six ounces.

Six silver forks and their silver tea-spoons, the fifth part taken and weighing twelve ounces.

Three silver table spoons, weighing about two ounces.

One large silver fountain, engraved, one-fifth part taken and weighing twenty-three marks.

Another small silver fountain, engraved with vine-leaves, the one-fifth taken, weighing thirteen marks.

One silver deep bowl, for shaving purposes, the one-fifth taken and weighing twelve marks.

One large silver waiter, weighing fourteen ounces.

One silver basin, with my coat-of-arms, the one-fifth taken and weighing nine marks.

III. Text of that part of the will signed by Don Antonio José Ortiz on August 12, 1806, which refers to silver discussed in this study. Translated from original *Ortiz Family Papers*, Doc. No. 2, State Records and Archives, Santa Fe, New Mexico:

I declare for my heirs a service of table silver consisting of thirty plates and a complete set of six large plates. Twenty-four place settings of spoons [and forks] all with tax stamps. Twelve knives in addition to eleven place settings [forks and spoons] more. A salt cellar and tray and tureen. Two large spoons and a ladle, a set of vinegar cruets, two bowls [of thin metal] and three badly damaged tantaluses and two candlesticks.

IV. Text of that part of the will signed by Doña Rosa Bustamante, widow of retired Captain of Militia and Royal Alférez Don Antonio José Ortiz on July 9, 1814, which refers to silver discussed in this study. Translated from original *Ortiz Family Papers*, Doc. No. 3, State Records and Archives, Santa Fe, New Mexico:

Twenty-nine silver plates with tax marks . . . .

Thirty-four place settings [forks and spoons] of same . . . .

[with tax stamps] and two serving forks, one damaged . . . .

Two ladles of same [taxed] . . . .

One tureen of same [taxed] . . . .

One set of vinegar cruets of same [taxed] . . . .

Six large plates of same [taxed] . . . .

Two salt cellars of same [taxed] . . . .

Twelve knives of same [taxed] with one broken . . . .

Five common [without tax stamps] plates . . . .

Six place settings [forks and spoons] of same [without tax stamps] and one cheap fork . . . .

. . . .

Two damaged tantaluses and another basin . . . .

V. List of *Cajas Reales* approved by his Majesty the King of Spain in 1792. Copied from Anderson's *The Art of the Silversmith in Mexico 1519–1936*, Vol. I, p. 7:

1st. class: Mexico and Veracruz.

2nd class: Puebla, Guadalajara, Valladolid, San Luis Potosí, Durango, Zacatecas, Oaxaca, and Mérida de Yucatán.

3rd class: Bolaños, Zimapán, Pachuca, Acapulco, Chihuahua, el Rosario, Campeche, the disbursement office of Arizpe, and the *caja* of Cardonál.

Later the disbursement office of Saltillo was established.

INDEX

Walker Lithocraft Printing, Inc.
Tucson, Arizona